The Carer's Cookbook

Created by
Carolyn Peacock

Inspired by
Angela Hamlin

Foreword by
Joanna Lumley

Draycott Nursing

First published in 2001
by Carolyn Peacock

©Carolyn Peacock, July 2001

ISBN 0-9541024-0-1

A CIP catalogue of this book is
available from the British Library.

Design by Moving Brands
www.movingbrands.com

Typeset by Brad Yendle
studio@designtypography.com

Grateful thanks to John Burman of Hewitson
Becke + Shaw, Solicitors, Cambridge, Ian Jarvis
of ACR Computer Systems in Stamford,
Dean Simpole-Clarke of Simpole Clarke in Stamf
Scott Marsden BSc., SRD., Senior Dietician of the
London Clinic, James Bull, Ben Wolstenholme,
& Brad Yendle of Moving Brands and lastly in
alphabetical order kind friends and cooks who
have looked at the recipes Audrey Kisby, Tricia L
Tracey Palmer-Hall of Thyme Lords Catering
Company, Judy Skene and Susie Wingfield.

Contents

Preface
Carolyn Peacock

When Angela Hamlin of Draycott Nursing, mentioned that she wanted to produce a recipe book to help nurses and carers cook for their patients I spontaneously said, 'I would love to do that'.

The idea has snowballed from there and the more I thought about it the more we realised how incredibly important and worthwhile the project would be, not only for the benefit of the carer or patient/client, but for anyone who is looking after a loved one.

The aim of the book is to give ideas and inspire confidence. After all cookery is only interpretation and improvisation. It must be daunting to enter the home of a stranger and to be expected to care for them, as well as cook.

This cookbook will help the nurse/carer provide healthy and appetising meals. In order to simplify things we decided to give a monthly menu with additions. Obviously, no one can manage to work his or her way through all the menus, but it is a guide.

I would like to thank my husband Michael for his endless patience in helping me get the recipes onto the computer; and my Mother and daughters Charlotte and Emma, who together with Michael and our friends have been testing my various experiments which have led to these recipes. *'Bon appétit!'*

Carolyn Peacock

Introduction
Angela Hamlin

Having spent the majority of my career in hospitals I have always realised how important meals are to patients not only for the obvious reasons of building up the patient and following surgery repairing tissue, but as an important break in the day, causing a diversion in the often enforced monotony of the day.

This is no different when looking after patients in their own homes. At times the importance of meals are also part of treatment or recuperation. The aim is to provide a healthy diet. A 'healthy' diet is one, which provides all the essential nutrients in the correct quantities to avoid health problems associated with nutrient excesses or deficiencies.

At times our carers/nurses have been asked to cook extremely complicated dishes and I have to remind people we are not a catering agency.

The need for a recipe book became so apparent when interviewing a prospective carer/nurse. When asked what their cooking skills were like, on numerous occasions they said they were very good cooks. On delving deeper their repertoire often consisted of cooking sausages or stir-fry! I decided then that something needed to be done.

I am extremely grateful to Carolyn Peacock firstly for accepting the challenge, and then for the enormous amount of hard work and devotion she has put into '*The Carer's Cookbook*'.

A sincere thanks to Joanna Lumley for so graciously and generously agreeing to write the foreword to the book, knowing how busy she is, her time has been invaluable.

My thanks to my office team and good friends Lynda Berry and Sally Bulloch who have all contributed enormously with their advice and considered opinions.

Angela Hamlin.

Foreword
Joanna Lumley

When I was first asked to write a foreword to *'The Carer's Cookbook'*, I responded immediately by saying, 'What a delicious and good idea! I'd be so proud to be connected with this excellent venture'.

The role of the carer is unique and takes into account every aspect of a patient's life. Producing appetising meals must be essential in nursing a person back to health. Having so often come across people who need care at home, I fully appreciate how important meals are to those who are confined to their home.

The aim of this book is to be an easy reference book to those in the caring profession. The carers have often not had formal cookery training.

I am delighted that profits from the sale of the book will go towards sponsoring training days for carers.

To quote George Bernard Shaw (1856-1950), 'There is no love sincerer than the love of food'.

I wish this book every success.

Joanna Lumley.

Conversion charts
Solids & liquids

Approximate conversion measures for solids

OUNCES (OZ) *to* GRAMS (g)

1.0	25	10.0	275
2.0	50	12.0	325
3.0	75	12.5	350
4.0	100	13.0	375
4.5	125	14.0	400
5.0	150	15.0	425
6.0	175	16.0 (1LB)	450
8.0	225	1.5LBS	700
9.0	250	2.0LBS	1.0KG

Approximate conversion measures for liquids

FLUID OUNCES (FL.OZ) *to* MILLILITRES (ML)

1.0	25
2.0	50
3.0	75
4.0	100
4.0	125
5.0 (0.25PT)	150
6.0	175
7.0	200
8.0	225
10.0 (0.5PT)	275
10.5	300
20.0 (1.0PT)	575

Conversion charts
Oven temperatures

Oven temperature conversion

DEGREES (°C) *to* DEGREES (°F) *to* GAS MARK

VERY COOL

130°C	250°F	*gas mark* 0.5
140°C	275°F	*gas mark* 1

COOL

150°C	300°F	*gas mark* 2

WARM

170°C	325°F	*gas mark* 3

MODERATE

180°C	350°F	*gas mark* 4

FAIRLY HOT

190°C	375°F	*gas mark* 5
200°C	400°F	*gas mark* 6

HOT

220°C	425°F	*gas mark* 7

VERY HOT

230°C	450°F	*gas mark* 8
240°C	475°F	*gas mark* 9
250°C	500°F	*gas mark* 10

* optional

Conversion charts
Roasting times for
turkey & stuffing

Roasting times for turkey

15-20 minutes on 220°C or 425°F or gas mark 7.
Lower heat to 180°C or 350°F or gas mark 4 for
remainder of roasting time. (2LBS = 1KG)

WEIGHT (LBS & KG) *to* HOURS

5 - 6	2.2 - 2.6	3.0 - 3.5
6 - 8	2.6 - 3.5	3.5 - 4.0
8 - 10	3.5 - 4.5	4.0 - 4.5
10 - 12	4.5 - 5.3	4.5 - 5.0
12 - 15	5.3 - 6.7	5.0 - 5.5
15 - 17	6.7 - 7.6	5.5 - 6.0
17 - 20	7.6 - 9.0	6.0 - 6.5
20 - 25	9.0 - 11.2	6.5 - 7.0

Quantities of stuffing for turkey

WEIGHT *to* QUANTITY

(LBS)	(KG)	(OZ & LBS)	(G & KG)
5 - 6	2.2 - 2.6	10.0 - 12.0	275 - 325
6 - 8	2.6 - 3.5	12.0 - 1.0	325 - 450
8 - 10	3.5 - 4.5	1.00 - 1.50	450 - 700
10 - 12	4.5 - 5.3	1.50 - 1.75	700 - 800
12 - 15	5.3 - 6.7	1.75 - 2.00	800 - 1.00
15 - 17	6.7 - 7.6	2.00 - 2.50	1.00 - 1225
17 - 20	7.6 - 9.0	2.50 - 3.00	1225- 1350
20 - 25	9.0 - 11.2	3.00 - 4.00	1350- 1800

Useful information
Cooking meat

Oven cooking times for meat

BEEF

10-15 minutes per LB (450g)
220°C or 425°F or gas mark7

LAMB

20 minutes per LB (450g)
230°C or 450°F or gas mark 8 *add* extra 20 minutes

PORK

30 minutes per LB (450g)
230°C or 450°F or gas mark 8 *add* extra 30 minutes

ROAST CHICKEN

2-3.5LB (1-1.5KG) bird
190-200°C or 375-400°F or gas mark 5-6 for 50-100
minutes. Pierce thigh. If juice runs clear and there is
no blood, chicken is cooked. Pre-heat oven and melt
butter or vegetable fat spread and olive oil or
sunflower seed oil in roasting tin. Put meat into
hot fat. Juices run from the meat during cooking.
The goodness from the meat is used to make gravy.

GRAVY

Pour fat from roasting tin into a heatproof container.
Leave rich brown juices at the bottom of the roasting
tin. Sprinkle 1oz (25g) flour over pan juices. Stir with
wooden spoon and blend in half a pint (275ML) of
stock or water until gravy is smooth. Gravy granules
can be added at this stage. Individual taste dictates
consistency of gravy. Season to taste. Strain gravy
into a sauceboat. If there are good rich pan juices
left in the roasting tin, gravy can be made by adding
stock or water. Gravy made without flour is lighter
and thinner.

PORK CRACKLING

Score fat with sharp knife. Sprinkle with salt.
Baste with hot fat. Add more salt towards the
end of roasting.

Useful information
Cooking eggs

FRIED EGG

Heat butter or vegetable fat spread in pan. Break egg into pan. Fry until egg white is just set.

HARD BOILED EGG

Bring pan of water to boil. Simmer egg for 10 minutes. Put egg in cold water after cooking.

POACHED EGG

Bring shallow pan of water to boil. Add 1 teaspoon of vinegar. (This helps hold egg white together). Break egg and slip into boiling water. Simmer for 3-4 minutes. Remove with slotted spoon.

SCRAMBLED EGG

Break eggs into a bowl. Beat well and add 2oz (50g) melted butter or vegetable fat spread. Pour into saucepan. Cook on low heat until just set. Do not overcook.

SOFT BOILED EGG

Bring pan of water to boil. Add egg. Reduce heat. Simmer for 3 minutes.

Eggs can harbour bacteria, especially Salmonellae, which penetrate the eggs through cracks in the shell. Some eggs may be infected that are flawless in appearance. In recipes that require raw eggs, or softly cooked eggs please always use fresh eggs. People with low resistance i.e. pregnant mothers or the elderly can be affected.

Useful information
Cooking fish

BAKING

Place fish in ovenproof dish. Dot with knobs of
butter. Cover with silver foil and bake in pre-heated
oven on 180-190°C or 350-375°F or gas mark 4-5 for
15 minutes.

FRYING

Heat butter or vegetable fat spread in frying pan.
Dip fish in beaten egg and then in mixture of flour
and breadcrumbs. Fry 4 minutes each side. With
thicker cuts of fish, char-grill on a ridged steak pan.

GRILLING

Brush fish with melted butter or vegetable fat spread.
Place on silver foil in grill pan. Grill for
4 minutes each side.

POACHING

Salmon or individual pieces of fish. Put fish in pan.
Cover with water Bring to the boil for 1 minute.
Remove from heat. Leave fish to cool in water.
Fish will be cooked and moist.

STEAMING

Place fish on a plate. Cover with silver foil.
Put covered plate over a saucepan of boiling water
and steam for 15 minutes.

Useful information
Cooking potatoes

ANNA POTATOES

Line cake tin with greaseproof paper. Peel and thinly slice potatoes. Place in overlapping layers in cake tin. Season to taste. Add 2oz (50g) melted butter or vegetable fat spread. Cover with greaseproof paper. Bake for about 1 hour on 190°C or 375°F or gas mark 5. If potatoes become too dry, add extra butter or vegetable fat spread. Turn out onto serving dish.

BAKED POTATOES

Serve with butter or vegetable fat spread or fromage frais or sour cream or grated cheese or baked beans or finely chopped chicken or chopped ham etc. Wash potatoes. Dry and rub with olive oil and salt. Bake on 180-190°C or 350-375°F or gas mark 4-5 for 1 hour or until soft. Slice top of potato and insert flavouring.

DUCHESS POTATOES

Boil potatoes for 5-10 minutes. Mash and beat in butter or vegetable fat spread and 1 beaten egg. The mixture should be smooth and dry. Add nutmeg. Season to taste. Use a dessertspoon to shape potato into rounds or put into piping bag and squeeze through a nozzle. Lay potato on baking tray. Bake on 200°C or 400°F or gas mark 6 until crisp and brown.

FRIED POTATOES

Peel potatoes. Cut into small cubes. Melt 2oz (50g) butter or vegetable fat spread and 1 tablespoon olive oil. Heat until foaming. Add potatoes. Fry until crisp and brown on both sides. Drain on absorbent kitchen paper.

MASHED POTATOES

Peel potatoes. Slice and boil for 5-10 minutes. Mash and add butter or vegetable fat spread and a little milk. Beat until smooth. Season to taste.

NEW POTATOES

Scrub off any dirt. Boil for 5-10 minutes. Drain. Return to pan and toss in 1oz (25g) butter or vegetable fat spread, chopped parsley and chopped mint.

Useful information
Cooking vegetables

ASPARAGUS

Cut off woody end of asparagus and wash in cold water. Tie asparagus in a bundle. Place in upright position in a narrow pan. Fill pan with boiling water to half way up asparagus stem. Cover and steam for 10-15 minutes. Serve with melted butter or vegetable fat spread or hollandaise sauce.

BEETROOT

Serve hot or cold. Buy raw or buy cooked in a vacuum pack. (PRECOOKED) To serve cold, simply add a vinaigrette dressing and sprinkle with parsley. To serve hot, slice thinly and cover with a white sauce sprinkled with breadcrumbs or cover with sour cream. Season to taste. (UNCOOKED) Wash beetroots. Do not trim or damage skin, otherwise beetroot will 'bleed' during cooking. Wrap in silver foil and put in ovenproof dish. Bake on 170°C or 325°F or gas mark 3 for 2 hours. When beetroot is cooked the skin comes off easily.

BRAISED FENNEL WITH TOMATOES AND GARLIC

Melt butter or vegetable fat spread in large saucepan. Slice fennel bulbs and add garlic. Sauté for 10 minutes. Season to taste. Add chopped tomatoes and 1 teaspoon lemon juice. Simmer for 10 minutes.

BROAD BEANS

If broad beans are large, remove skin. Boil for 7 minutes and drain. Serve tossed in butter or vegetable fat spread. Sprinkle with chopped parsley.

BROCCOLI

Separate broccoli into florets about 2 inches in length. Discard coarse stem. Boil for 5-7 minutes. Season to taste. Toss in butter or vegetable fat spread. Sprinkle with toasted breadcrumbs.

BRUSSELS SPROUTS

Remove outer leaves. Cut across bottom of sprout. Place in boiling water for 7-10 minutes. Do not overcook. Drain and toss in melted butter or vegetable fat spread. Season to taste.

CARROTS

Juice and rind half a lemon, 1 teaspoon soft brown sugar, 1oz (25g) butter or vegetable fat spread and 1 tablespoon chopped mint. Trim and scrub carrots. Boil for 5-7 minutes and drain. Put in saucepan with butter or vegetable fat spread, sugar and mint. Toss over a high heat for a couple of minutes.

CAULIFLOWER

Remove stem and outside leaves. Boil in covered pan for 5-10 minutes and drain. Serve with a teaspoon melted butter or vegetable fat spread. Season to taste. Cover with a cheese sauce or sprinkle with chopped parsley.

COURGETTES

Top and tail courgettes. (Use miniature yellow or green marrow). Cut lengthways or across. Boil or sauté in 1oz (25g) butter or vegetable fat spread for 5 minutes. Add a squeeze of lemon juice. Season to taste.

CREAMED PARSNIPS

Peel and chop parsnips and boil for 7 minutes. Drain and purée in a food processor. Season to taste. Stir in 1 tablespoon of single cream.

FRENCH/RUNNER/HARICOT VERT BEANS

Wash beans. Top and tail. Slice diagonally in thin strips. Boil 7-10 minutes.

GREEN CABBAGE

Cut off thick stalk and discoloured outer leaves. Slice or shred in thin strips. Boil for 4-6 minutes. Drain and toss in butter or vegetable fat spread. Season to taste. Add a pinch of ground nutmeg.*

GREEN PEAS

Shell peas. Boil for 4-5 minutes. Drain and toss in melted butter or vegetable fat spread and freshly chopped mint.

LEEKS

Cut leeks in half. Wash thoroughly in water.
Cut leeks in rounds. Melt butter or vegetable fat
spread in saucepan. Add leeks and sauté for 10
minutes. Season to taste. Serve in cooking juices.

MUSHROOMS

Wash and peel mushrooms. Sauté in melted butter
or vegetable fat spread for 5-10 minutes. Drain and
season with salt and freshly ground pepper.

RED CABBAGE

1 onion, 3 tablespoons soft brown sugar, salt, freshly
ground pepper and half to a 1 pint (575ML) red wine
or stock. Sauté sliced onion in butter or vegetable fat
spread until transparent. Add finely shredded red
cabbage. (Discard stalk and outer leaves). Season to
taste. Add sugar and enough red wine or stock to
cover. Simmer on low heat for 1 hour.

SPINACH

Wash spinach. Strip leaves off stalk. Put in saucepan.
Simmer with 2 tablespoons of water in covered pan
for 3-5 minutes. Leaves will wilt. Drain off water.
Season to taste. Add a tablespoon of single cream.

STUFFED TOMATOES

Cut tomatoes in half. Remove seeds and juice.
Mix breadcrumbs, garlic, chopped parsley, basil,*
juice and seeds of tomatoes. Mash with a little
melted butter or vegetable fat spread. Season to taste.
Replace mixture in tomatoes and place in a shallow
baking dish. Bake on 180°C or 350°F or gas mark 4
for 10 minutes until tomatoes are tender and
breadcrumbs are brown.

*optional

28 day section
3 recipes per day

01

Light meal
Celery in cream
Serves two

1 bunch of young celery – trimmed & cut into thin strips
half a pint (275ml) single cream
half a teaspoon of ground nutmeg
salt & freshly ground pepper
2 garlic cloves – squeezed*
4oz (100g) toasted breadcrumbs
2oz (50g) butter

Instructions

1. Preheat oven 180°C or 350°F or gas mark 4.

2. Place strips of celery in ovenproof dish.

3. Mix together cream, nutmeg, salt, freshly ground pepper and if using, garlic.

4. Pour cream over celery. Sprinkle with toasted breadcrumbs and dot with knobs of butter. Bake in a preheated oven for half an hour until celery is tender and breadcrumbs are brown.

   Celery is equally delicious covered in white wine & braised in the oven.

   Serve with slices of ham.

*optional

**Light meal
Celery in cream
Serves two**

**Main meal
Poached chicken
in parsley sauce
Serves two**

**Pudding
Hot lemon pudding
Serves two/four**

Day 01

Pudding
Hot lemon pudding
Serves two/four

3oz (75g) self raising flour
8oz (225g) sugar
half a pint (275ml) milk (full or low fat)
2 large eggs – separated
grated rind & juice of 1 lemon
small pinch salt
whipped cream to serve

1. Lightly grease a 1 pint (575ML) ovenproof dish.
   Preheat oven 170°C or 325°F or gas mark 3.

2. Sift together flour and sugar in a mixing bowl.

3. Add milk, beaten egg yolks, lemon juice, rind
   and a pinch of salt and stir.

4. Whisk egg whites until very stiff and fold them
   into the lemon mixture, using a metal spoon.

5. Pour into a buttered baking dish.

6. Set baking dish in a baking tin with 1 inch of water
   in the bottom of tin.

7. Bake in a preheated oven for 35-40 minutes.
   The pudding should be firm on top, light and fluffy
   underneath and be surrounded by lemon sauce.

   Serve warm with a bowl of whipped cream.

Main meal
Poached chicken
in parsley sauce
Serves two

1 small chicken
4 carrots — peeled & roughly chopped
1 onion — peeled & cut into four
1 parsnip — peeled & roughly chopped
2oz (50g) butter
2oz (50g) flour
1 large bunch of parsley — chopped very fine
salt & freshly ground pepper
cream to taste

1. Place chicken and vegetables in a large saucepan. Cover with water.

2. Bring to the boil. Lower heat and simmer in covered pan for 45 minutes.

3. Leave chicken in stock until completely cold.

4. Remove chicken from stock. Strip off flesh and cut into bite sized pieces.

5. Replace chicken carcass and bones in stock. Simmer for 1 hour. Leave until cold. Skim fat from surface of stock. Strain stock through sieve.

6. To make parsley sauce, melt 2oz (50g) butter or vegetable fat spread in a small saucepan and blend in flour. Stir constantly and gradually whisk in half a pint (275ML) chicken stock. Stir until smooth and lump free. Add chopped parsley. Season to taste. Add a touch of cream.*

7. Pour parsley sauce over chicken and reheat in medium oven.

   Serve with rice and garden peas.

02

Light meal
Spanish potato
omelette
Serves four

*Ingredients
& preparation*

4oz (100g) butter or vegetable fat spread
1 red onion – peeled & finely chopped
1lb (450g) potatoes – peeled & cut in very small cubes
2 small red peppers – cut in small pieces
1 courgette – cut in small pieces
1 stick of celery – sliced & cut into small pieces
4oz (100g) frozen peas
2oz (50g) cheddar cheese
3 tablespoons chopped parsley
6 large eggs
1 clove garlic – squeezed*
salt & freshly ground pepper

Instructions

1. Heat 2oz (50g) butter or vegetable fat spread in large frying pan and sauté onion until soft. Add potatoes, peppers, courgettes and celery. Sauté a further 4 minutes on a low heat. Add thawed peas. Season to taste. Stir in the cheese and the parsley.

2. Beat eggs and season well with salt and black pepper. Pour them over the vegetables. Stir well.

3. Pour mixture into a large heated omelette pan containing 2oz melted butter or vegetable fat spread. Move mixture round with fork to ensure liquid is evenly distributed. Cook until eggs are beginning to set.

4. Remove from heat and place omelette in pan under a hot grill until omelette is light brown.

5. Slide spatula round omelette and transfer to serving dish.

   Equally good hot or cold. Serve cut in slices, with a green salad.

*optional

18.

**Light meal
Spanish potato
omelette
Serves four**

**Main meal
Baked sausages
Serves two**

**Pudding
Melon & passion
fruit in fruit juice
Serves two**

Pudding
Melon & passion
fruit in fruit juice
Serves two

1 honeydew melon
1 galia melon
4 passion fruits
quarter of a pint (150ml) fresh lime or orange juice
2 tablespoons chopped mint
6 sponge fingers
sugar to taste*

1. Cut melons in half and remove seeds.

2. Using a melon baller, scoop out melon flesh into small balls and place in a serving bowl.

3. Cut passion fruit in half. Scoop out seeds and juice with a teaspoon and add to the melon balls.

4. Cover with lime or orange juice.

5. Sprinkle with chopped mint. Cover and chill in fridge for 2 hours.

   Serve with 2-3 sponge fingers.

Main meal
Baked sausages
Serves two

(METHOD A)
1 packet of good quality pork sausages
1 tin of tomato or bolognese sauce

or

(METHOD B)
1 onion – peeled & sliced
1oz (25g) butter
2 large eating apples – cored, peeled & chopped
3 sticks celery – finely chopped
half a pint (275ml) cider
1 vegetable stock cube
1 tablespoon brown sugar
1 teaspoon soy sauce
salt & freshly ground pepper

1. Preheat oven 190° C or 375°F or gas mark 5.

2. Prick sausages with fork and place in baking tin.

3. Cook sausages in a preheated oven until crisp and brown. Drain off fat. Put sausages in an ovenproof dish.

4. (METHOD A) Pour tomato or bolognese sauce over sausages and return to the oven for 20 minutes to a half an hour.

5. (METHOD B) Sauté onion in the butter until soft. Add apples, and celery, cider, stock cube, brown sugar and soy sauce. Season to taste and stir well.

6. Pour cider sauce over sausages. Bake on 180°C or 350°F or gas mark 4 for 20 minutes to a half an hour.

    Serve with a baked potato and courgettes.

Light meal
Hot avocados
with bacon
Serves one

4 slices bacon
1 avocado
2 tablespoons single cream
2 tablespoons grated cheddar cheese

1. Preheat oven 190° C or 375°F or gas mark 5.

2. Cut bacon into small pieces and fry until crisp.

3. Cut the avocado in half and remove the stone. Scoop out avocado flesh and mash with cream and bacon.

4. Pile mixture into avocado skins and place on a baking tray.

5. Sprinkle with cheese and bake in a preheated oven for 10 minutes.

   Serve with brown wholemeal bread.

   An alternative to flavouring with bacon could be to use 2oz (50g) finely chopped chicken or prawns.

*optional

**Light meal
Hot avocados
with bacon
Serves one**

**Main meal
Salmon pie
Serves four**

**Pudding
Berries on bread
Serves four**

Day 03

Pudding
Berries on bread
Serves four

1 punnet of strawberries
1 punnet of raspberries
1 punnet of blackcurrants or redcurrants
1 punnet of blueberries
2 tablespoons of brown sugar
4 thick slices of white bread – crusts removed
2 tablespoons of cassis*
cream or yoghurt to serve

1. Place fruit and sugar in saucepan.

2. Heat slowly to dissolve sugar and bring to the bo

3. Remove from heat and add cassis. Taste and add more sugar if needed. Cool for 10 minutes.

4. Arrange bread slices on serving plates. Spoon fruit onto bread.

   Serve with cream or yoghurt.

   The soft fruits will produce liquid, therefore the cassis is optional.

Main meal
Salmon pie
Serves four

1lb (450g) frozen puff pastry
2 × 1lb (900g) salmon fillets – skinned
4oz (100g) long grain rice
half a pint (275ml) fish or chicken stock cube
2oz (50g) unsalted butter or vegetable fat spread
6 spring onions – finely chopped
4oz (100g) mushrooms – sliced
3 hard boiled eggs – shelled & chopped
1 teaspoon fresh parsley
1 teaspoon chopped fresh tarragon
1 beaten egg
salt & freshly ground pepper
quarter of a pint (150ml) sour cream
1 glass of dry white wine*

1. Preheat oven 220° C or 425°F or gas mark 7.

2. Put pastry on one side to thaw.

3. Cook rice in the chicken or fish stock. Melt butter or vegetable fat spread and sauté spring onions and mushrooms for 2 minutes. Leave to cool.

4. Place fish in a saucepan. Cover with water and white wine if using. Bring to the boil. Remove saucepan from heat. Leave fish to cool in liquid. Remove fish from liquid, place in a bowl and carefully flake into small pieces, discarding all bones. Combine rice, mushrooms, onion and hard boiled eggs and add to the fish. Stir in parsley and tarragon. Season to taste.

5. Cut pastry in half and roll each half into a long rectangular shape. Line a baking tin with greaseproof paper. Lay one half of pastry on greaseproof paper. Cover pastry with salmon filling to within 1 inch of the edge. Cover with second sheet of pastry.

6. Dampen edges of pastry with water and press together. Cut small air vents in top of pastry at intervals of 1 inch with a small knife. Leave to rest for 30 minutes.

7. Brush the pie with a beaten egg. Bake in a preheated oven for 30 minutes, or until pastry is risen and golden, and transfer to serving dish.

   Serve with a green salad and a large bowl of sour cream.

04

Light meal
Baked mushrooms
Serves two

2 large flat mushrooms – wiped clean
2oz (50g) butter or vegetable fat spread – melted
4oz (100g) blue brie or cambozola cheese – diced
1 lemon
salt & freshly ground pepper

1. Preheat oven 190° C or 375°F or gas mark 5.

2. Brush mushrooms with melted butter or vegetabl
   fat spread. Season with salt, pepper and lemon jui

3. Bake in oven for 5 minutes.

4. Put diced cheese inside the mushrooms. Return t
   the oven and bake for 10 minutes. The mushroom
   should be tender and the cheese melted.

   Serve with warm crusty bread and a green salad.

*optional

**Light meal
Baked mushrooms
Serves two**

**Main meal
Chicken in
tarragon sauce
Serves two**

**Pudding
Crème caramel
Serves four**

Day 04

Pudding
Crème caramel
Serves four

2oz (50g) granulated sugar
4 tablespoons water
4 eggs
1oz (25g) caster sugar
1 pint (575ml) milk or single cream (or low fat)
1 teaspoon of vanilla essence

1. Preheat oven 150° C or 300°F or gas mark 2.

2. Dissolve 2oz sugar in 4 tablespoons of water on lo
   heat. Boil until liquid becomes a rich caramel colo
   Pour syrup into a soufflé dish, it will harden on
   contact with the dish.

3. Beat together eggs and 1oz (25g) caster sugar.
   Heat milk or cream until just warm and pour ove
   eggs. Add vanilla essence and whisk well. Strain
   custard into soufflé dish.

4. Place soufflé dish in baking tin containing 1 inch
   of water. Cover soufflé dish with silver foil.

5. Bake in pre-heated oven until custard is set – abo
   an hour. (Top of custard should be firm to the tou
   Chill for 4 hours or longer.

   To turn out ease a knife between the crème caramel
   and the soufflé dish. Put a deep sided plate on top
   of soufflé dish. Holding onto plate and soufflé dish,
   invert the crème caramel onto plate. The crème caramel
   will be surrounded by caramel sauce and will be brown
   on top.

Main meal Chicken in tarragon sauce Serves two

2 skinless chicken breasts – cut into small pieces
half a red onion – peeled & sliced
2oz (50g) butter or vegetable fat spread
2 tablespoons of dry white wine
2 tablespoons fresh or dried tarragon
4 tablespoons of crème fraiche or low fat cream cheese
2 teaspoons of lemon juice
1 tablespoon chopped parsley
salt & freshly ground pepper

1. Melt butter or vegetable fat spread and sauté onion until soft.

2. Add the chicken and simmer for 5-7 minutes, seasoning well.

3. Add wine, tarragon, crème fraiche or low fat cream cheese. Season to taste. Bring to simmering point.

4. Remove from heat and add lemon juice to taste.

5. Sprinkle with chopped parsley.

   Serve with new potatoes and peas.

Light meal
Prawn, rice
& avocado salad
Serves two

4oz (100g) mange tout
8oz (225g) large cooked & peeled prawns
6oz (175g) cooked white rice
2 spring onions – chopped
2 avocados – peeled & chopped
1 green pepper – sliced

(DRESSING)
3 large tablespoons mayonnaise
2 tablespoons single cream
2 tablespoons chopped dill
2 tablespoons of white wine*

1. Mix together mayonnaise, cream and dill.

2. Plunge mange tout in boiling water for 1 minute and drain well.

3. Mix prawns, rice, pepper, spring onions, avocados and mange tout. Add white wine.*

4. Stir 2 tablespoons of the dressing into the salad and serve the rest separately.

   Garnish with lettuce leaves and herbs.

**Light meal
Prawn, rice
& avocado salad
Serves two**

**Main meal
Shepherd's pie
Serves two**

**Pudding
Creamed rice
with apricot sauce
Serves two**

Day 05

Pudding
Creamed rice
with apricot sauce
Serves two

1 pint (575ml) milk
2oz (50g) pudding rice
2 tablespoons caster sugar
vanilla essence
quarter of a pint (150ml) double cream

(APRICOT SAUCE)
4oz (100g) dried apricots — soaked overnight in water
2 teaspoons lemon juice

1. Heat milk in a medium saucepan and add rice. Bring to the boil, lower heat and simmer for 10 minutes. Stir to prevent lumps forming. Top up with extra milk if needed.

2. Add sugar and a few drops of vanilla essence and leave to cool for 10 minutes.

3. Stir cream into cooked rice.

4. (APRICOT SAUCE) Simmer apricots in enough water to cover for 10 minutes.

5. Purée until smooth. Add sugar and lemon juice to taste.

   Serve apricot sauce separately.

Main meal
Shepherd's pie
Serves two

1lb (450g) raw minced beef or lamb
2oz (50g) butter or vegetable fat spread
1 onion – peeled & sliced
6 carrots – peeled & sliced
2 leeks – washed, peeled & sliced
quarter of a pint (150ml) stock (use stock cube)
1 tablespoon Worcester sauce
1 tablespoon tomato sauce
1 teaspoon soy sauce
2lbs (1kg) potatoes
1 beaten egg
salt & freshly ground pepper

1. Preheat oven 190° C or 375°F or gas mark 5.

2. Sauté onion in 1oz (25g) butter or vegetable fat spread.

3. Add minced meat, carrots and leeks to onion and simmer for 5 minutes until soft. Add the stock, Worcester, tomato and soy sauce. Season to taste.

4. Peel and boil potatoes for 10 minutes. Drain thoroughly and mash until completely smooth. Beat in butter and egg with a wooden spoon. If potato mixture is too thick, add a little milk.

5. Put meat mixture in pie-dish. Cover with mashed potatoes. Smooth potatoes and decorate in a criss-cross pattern using a fork. A little grated cheese on top of the potatoes adds to the flavour.

6. Bake in preheated oven for 30 minutes until potato is crisp and brown.

Serve with peas.

Light meal
Cheese soufflé
Serves two

Ingredients
preparation

2oz (50g) butter or vegetable fat spread
dry white breadcrumbs
1oz (25g) flour
half a teaspoon dried English mustard
half a pint (275ml) milk
4 eggs – separated
3 teaspoons of cayenne pepper
3oz (75g) mature cheddar or gruyere or blue cheese
salt & freshly ground pepper

Instructions

1. Preheat oven 200° C or 400°F or gas mark 6.

2. Pour a little melted butter round inside of soufflé dish and dust with breadcrumbs.

3. Melt butter or vegetable fat spread in a saucepan. Stir in flour, mustard and cayenne pepper. Blend in milk stirring with a wooden spoon – the mixture should get very thick and leave the sides of the pan Add cheese. Remove from heat and cool.

4. Beat in egg yolks, salt and pepper.

5. Whisk the egg whites until stiff. Whisk half of the egg whites into the cheese mixture, fold the remainder in using a metal spoon.

6. Bake for 20-30 minutes. Do not open oven door for the first 15 minutes of cooking the soufflé and then only if necessary, otherwise the soufflé will not rise

Serve with a mixed salad.

*optional

Light meal
Cheese soufflé
Serves two

Main meal
Roast chicken
Serves two

Pudding
Prune whip
Serves two

Pudding
Prune whip
Serves two

8oz (225g) prunes
5oz (150g) plain yoghurt
2 tablespoons runny honey
half a pint (275ml) double cream – lightly whipped
1 tablespoon almonds – toasted & chopped*

1. Cover prunes with water and simmer for 15
   minutes until tender.

2. Purée prunes and cooking liquor in food processor
   or rub through a sieve and leave to cool.

3. Mix together prune purée, yoghurt, honey and
   lightly whipped cream.

4. Spoon into glass dishes and decorate with chopped
   nuts. The almonds are optional, as some people
   have strong allergies to any types of nuts.

Main meal
Roast chicken
Serves two

1 medium sized chicken
3-4 rashers of bacon
1oz (25g) butter or vegetable fat spread
2 tablespoons plain flour
salt & freshly ground pepper

1. Preheat oven 200° C or 400°F or gas mark 6.

2. Season chicken and cover with rashers of bacon.

3. Heat butter or vegetable fat spread in roasting tin.

4. Put chicken in roasting tin. Roast for 45 minutes in a preheated oven. The chicken will be cooked when juices from leg run clear showing no traces of blood.

5. Remove bacon 15 minutes before the end of cooking. Sprinkle flour over chicken breast.

6. Baste chicken. Return to oven for 15 minutes until skin is brown and crisp.

7. Put the chicken on a serving dish in a warm place. To make the gravy pour fat out of roasting tin. Sprinkle a little flour over pan juices and stir with wooden spoon. Add enough stock or water for required thickness. Stir until smooth. Season to taste.

8. Strain gravy into sauceboat.

    Serve with boiled potatoes, carrots and bread sauce.

    See page 120 of the sauce section in rear of book for the recipe for bread sauce.

7

Light meal
Melon & parma ham
with melba toast
Serves two

ingredients
preparation

1 sweet cantaloupe, galia or honeydew melon
6 thin slices parma ham
2-3 leaves of fresh mint
freshly ground pepper

(MELBA TOAST)
1 packet of thick sliced bread

instructions

1. Skin and remove pips from melon. Slice thinly and put on a serving dish.

2. Cover melon with slices of parma ham.

3. Decorate with leaves of fresh mint.

4. (MELBA TOAST) Toast bread on both sides. Cut off crusts.

5. Slice toast in two diagonally. Gently peel away any un-cooked bread from inside of toast.

6. Put toast in oven on 140°C or 275°F or gas mark for an hour. Toast should curl up and become light brown on both sides.

   Keeps for weeks if stored in an airtight tin.

**Light meal
Melon & parma ham
with melba toast
Serves two**

**Main meal
Ham & asparagus
in cheese sauce
Serves two**

**Pudding
Apple snow
Serves two**

Day 07

Pudding
Apple snow
Serves two

1lb (450g) cooking apples
2 oz (50g) caster sugar
8 egg whites
2 tablespoons water
grated rind & juice of half a lemon

1. Peel, core and slice apples and put in a pan.

2. Add water and sprinkle with sugar. Cover and simmer for 5-10 minutes until soft.

3. Purée apple in a food processor or pass through a sieve. Leave to cool.

4. Whisk egg whites until stiff and fold into apple purée. Mix in lemon juice and rind.

5. Spoon into glasses and leave to chill until ready to serve.

Main meal
Ham & asparagus
in cheese sauce
Serves two

(SAUCE)
2oz (50g) butter or vegetable fat spread
1oz (25g) plain flour
half a pint (275ml) milk
3oz (75g) grated cheddar or gruyere cheese
2 teaspoons Dijon mustard
salt & freshly ground pepper

8 large fresh or tinned asparagus spears
4 slices ham
4oz (100g) fresh white breadcrumbs

1. Preheat oven 190° C or 375°F or gas mark 5.

2. Melt butter or vegetable fat spread. Add flour and blend in milk. Stir until smooth. Add cheese and mustard. Season to taste.

3. Remove from heat and set aside.

4. Cut woody stems off asparagus.

5. Place asparagus in tall saucepan. Fill with boiling water to half way up asparagus stalks. Cover and boil for 4 minutes. The tips of the asparagus will cook in the steam.

6. Cut ham slices in half and wrap each piece around an asparagus spear. Put in baking dish.

7. Cover asparagus with cheese sauce. Sprinkle with breadcrumbs.

8. Bake in a preheated oven for 20 minutes, until top is brown and crisp.

   Serve with new potatoes and salad.

Light meal
Crusty rolls with egg o
smoked salmon filling
Serves two

2 soft white rolls or bagels

(EGG FILLING)
1 hardboiled egg – chopped
2 tablespoons mayonnaise
2 teaspoons chopped parsley
salt & freshly ground pepper
parsley sprigs to garnish

or

(SMOKED SALMON FILLING)
2oz (50g) smoked salmon – finely chopped
2oz (50g) cream cheese
1 teaspoon chopped chives
1 teaspoon lemon juice
freshly ground pepper
chives
salad leaves

1. Preheat oven 180°C or 350°F or gas mark 4.
   Heat rolls or bagels in oven until warm.

2. (EGG FILLING) Mix chopped eggs, mayonnaise and
   parsley. Season to taste. Cut roll in half and fill
   with egg mixture. Decorate with chopped parsley

3. (SMOKED SALMON FILLING) Mix cream cheese,
   chives, lemon juice and smoked salmon. Season
   with freshly ground pepper. Cut roll in half and
   fill with salmon mixture.

   Garnish with salad leaves and chopped chives.

Light meal
Crusty rolls with egg or smoked salmon filling
Serves two

Main meal
Chutney chicken
Serves two

Pudding
Baked raspberry creams
Serves two

Day 08

Pudding
Baked raspberry
creams
Serves two

2 eggs
2 egg yolks
sugar
8oz (225g) fresh or frozen raspberries
1 pint (575ml) carton double cream
fresh raspberries, strawberries or redcurrants
icing sugar to dust

1. Preheat oven 170°C or 325°F or gas mark 3.

2. Whisk together 2 eggs and 2 egg yolks.

3. Pureé raspberries and strain through sieve.

4. Add raspberries, sugar and double cream to egg mixture. Stir well.

5. Divide mixture between 6 ramekin dishes, or put into one soufflé dish.

6. Put dishes in baking tin containing 1 inch or (2.5CM) water.

7. Cover with greaseproof paper and bake in a prehe oven for 30 minutes, or until set. Chill overnight

   Dust with icing sugar before serving, and decora with fresh raspberries, strawberries or redcurrants

Main meal
Chutney chicken
Serves two

1 small chicken
2 tablespoons chopped chutney
3 tablespoons worcester sauce
1 teaspoon dried mustard
2 teaspoons dry curry powder
half a pint (275ml) whipping cream
8oz (225g) cooked rice
salt & freshly ground pepper
a few broccoli florets

1. Preheat oven 180°C or 350°F or gas mark 4.

2. Put chicken in saucepan and cover with water.
    Bring to the boil, then simmer for 1 hour.
    Leave chicken to cool in stock. Once cold remove
    chicken from stock, strip off flesh and cut into
    bite sized pieces.

3. Lightly whip cream. Fold in chopped chutney,
    worcester sauce, mustard and curry powder.
    Season to taste.

4. Pour sauce over chicken and bake in preheated
    oven for 15 minutes. Serve immediately on a bed
    of rice with broccoli florets.

5. Replace chicken carcass in stock. Bring to the boil
    and simmer for one hour. Cool, then refrigerate
    overnight. Skim fat off top of stock and strain stock
    through a sieve. Allow to cool.

    Fresh stock maybe decanted into small containers
    and frozen. Use stock for making soup.

9

Light meal
Potato & parsnip bake
Serves two

6 potatoes – peeled & sliced
4 parsnips – peeled & sliced
half a pint (275ml) single cream
2oz (50g) butter or vegetable fat spread
2-3 large tablespoons toasted breadcrumbs
salt & freshly ground pepper

1. Preheat oven 190°C or 350°F or gas mark 5.

2. Boil potatoes for 4 minutes. Drain (potatoes shoul be slightly hard in the middle). Boil parsnips for minutes. Drain (parsnips should be slightly hard in the middle).

3. Place the vegetables in layers in an ovenproof dish. Cover with cream and knobs of butter. Season to taste.

4. Cover with thick layer of breadcrumbs. Bake in a preheated oven for 30-35 minutes or until golden brown.

   Serve with granary bread.

Light meal
Potato & parsnip bake
Serves two

Main meal
Fried liver & bacon
Serves two

Pudding
Oranges in
caramel sauce
Serves two

Day 09

Pudding Oranges in caramel sauce Serves two

4 oranges
6oz (175g) sugar
a quarter pint (150ml) water
a few drops of vanilla essence
a tablespoon of orange liqueur*

1. Wash oranges.

2. Remove rind from oranges using a rind zester and reserve.

3. Peel pith from oranges.

4. Slice oranges with a sharp knife holding them ove a bowl to retain the juice.

5. (CARAMEL SYRUP) Melt sugar and water in a saucepan. Bring to the boil, lower heat and simme until syrup is golden brown and beginning to caramelise. Add a little water – it will hiss and ste – continue simmering until syrup has become run Then cool.

6. Pour the cooled syrup over the oranges. Add vanil essence and/or orange liqueur to taste.* Sprinkle with reserved zested orange rind.

Main meal
Fried liver & bacon
Serves two

8oz (225g) calves liver skinned & thinly sliced
4 slices of streaky bacon
1oz (25g) butter or vegetable fat spread
1 tablespoon of balsamic vinegar
salt & freshly ground pepper

1. Sauté or grill bacon in pan until crisp. Put to one side.

2. Heat butter or vegetable fat spread in frying pan. Fry liver 2 minutes each side. Should be brown on outside and pink in the middle.

3. Remove liver from pan. Drain away any fat and add 2 tablespoons of water and a tablespoon of balsamic vinegar to the pan juices. Season to taste. Pour gravy over liver and bacon.

   Serve with mashed potatoes and broad beans.

   or

1. (FOR WEIGHT WATCHERS) Place liver and bacon under a hot grill and grill for 2 minutes each side.

2. Serve sprinkled with chopped parsley.

   Serve with mashed potatoes and broad beans.

Light meal
Stuffed peppers
Serves four

4 peppers – green, yellow or red
1 lb (450g) pork sausages
2 tablespoons tomato purée
2 tablespoons chopped parsley
1 teaspoon mixed herbs
1 lb (450g) mushrooms – skinned & sliced
1 teacup of cooked rice
salt & freshly ground pepper
1 clove of garlic*

1. Preheat oven 190°C or 375°F or gas mark 5.

2. Cut off the top of the peppers. Scoop out seeds and white membrane.

3. Skin sausages. Purée sausage meat, tomato pureé and herbs. Season to taste.

4. Add the mushrooms to sausage meat, together with a teacup of cooked rice.

5. Fill peppers with sausage mixture and rice and replace top of the peppers.

6. Cover peppers with silver foil and bake in a preheated oven for 30 minutes.

   Serve on a bed of salad leaves.

*optional

Light meal
Stuffed peppers
Serves four

Main meal
Fish pie
Serves four

Pudding
Iced apricot brulée
Serves two

Day 10

Pudding
Iced apricot brulée
Serves two

large tin of apricots, peaches, or 8oz (225g) seedless grap
half a pint (275ml) double cream
3 tablespoons of soft brown sugar
*2 tablespoons of brandy**

1. Preheat grill to full heat.

2. Put fruit in soufflé dish.
   If using canned fruit drain off juice. Add brandy.*

3. Whisk cream. Spread over fruit.

4. Cover cream with a thick layer of soft brown sugar

5. Place under hot grill until sugar caramelises.

6. Serve immediately.

Main meal
Fish pie
Serves four

1lb (450g) firm white fish – cod or haddock
quarter of a pint (150ml) milk (low fat)
3oz (75g) butter or vegetable fat spread
2 tablespoons flour
3 hard boiled eggs – shelled & sliced
4 oz (100g) frozen peas
2 oz (50g) peeled prawns – fresh or frozen
half a teaspoon grated nutmeg
1lb (450g) potatoes
salt & freshly ground pepper

1. Preheat oven 180°C or 350°F or gas mark 4.

2. Skin fish and put in saucepan and cover with milk. Bring to the boil. Remove from heat and leave fish to infuse in the milk until cold.

3. Remove fish from milk and place in an ovenproof dish. Make a white sauce using fish flavoured milk. Melt 2oz (50g) butter or vegetable fat spread and stir constantly to blend in flour and the milk. Stir until sauce is thick and smooth. Use a wire whisk or wooden spoon. Season to taste.

4. Add fish, eggs, peas and prawns, to the white sauce. Season with nutmeg.

5. Peel and boil potatoes for 10 minutes. Drain. Mash and beat in 1oz (25g) butter or vegetable fat spread. Beat well. Season to taste. Spread mashed potato over fish mixture.

6. Bake in a preheated oven for 30-35 minutes or until dish is reheated and the potato is crisp and golden.

   Serve with mixed salad.

Light meal
Chicken, ham
salad club sandwich
Serves one

2oz (50g) chicken – cut into small pieces
1 tablespoon of mayonnaise
2 spring onions – finely chopped
2 slices of brown & 2 slices of white bread
1oz (25g) butter or vegetable fat spread
1 teaspoon whole grain mustard
1 slice of roast ham
1 sliced tomato & a few small salad leaves
salt & freshly ground pepper
4 cocktail sticks

1. Mix together chicken, mayonnaise and spring onic

2. Lightly butter 3 slices of bread.

3. Put mustard and ham on first slice of bread, chopp
   chicken on the second slice of bread and a layer of
   sliced tomato on the third slice of bread. Top each
   slice with small salad leaves. Sandwich together an
   finish with fourth slice of bread.

4. Cut sandwich into quarters, and secure with cockt
   sticks. Serve with potato crisps, mixed salad leaves
   and radishes.

Light meal
Chicken, ham
salad club sandwich
Serves one

Main meal
Moussaka
Serves two/four

Pudding
Treacle pudding
Serves two

Day 11

Pudding
Treacle pudding
Serves two

4oz (100g) butter or vegetable fat spread
4oz (100g) caster sugar
2 large eggs
4oz self-raising flour
4 tablespoons golden syrup

(TREACLE SAUCE)
4 tablespoons golden syrup
1 tablespoon water

1. Using an electric whisk beat butter and sugar together until light and fluffy.

2. Beat in eggs, one at a time and work in flour after having added second egg.

3. Butter a pint-sized (575ML) pudding basin. Spoon in golden syrup. Pour sponge mixture on top.

4. Cover top of pudding with buttered silver-foil, making a pleat across centre to allow pudding to

5. Steam for 1-2 hours in steamer or in large saucepan with pudding basin sitting on inverted saucer. Fill saucepan with boiling water to half way up side of pudding basin. Do not allow water to boil over top of pudding. Top up with boiling water from a kettle during steaming process.

6. (TREACLE SAUCE) Heat syrup and water in pan and serve in a sauceboat. Slide a knife between treacle pudding and pudding basin to loosen pudding. Invert onto wide-rimmed serving dish.

   Serve with custard or hot treacle sauce.

Main meal
Moussaka
Serves two/four

2 oz (50g) butter or vegetable fat spread
1 Spanish onion – peeled & sliced
1 clove garlic*
1 lb (450g) lamb – finely minced
4-6 tomatoes – seeded & chopped
8oz (225g) mushrooms – peeled & sliced
2 tablespoons chopped parsley
2 tablespoons tomato purée
4-6 tablespoons of beef stock
4 aubergines
6 tablespoons grated parmesan
flour
quarter of a pint (150ml) red wine*
salt & freshly ground pepper

1. Preheat oven 180°C or 350°F or gas mark 4.

1. Heat butter or vegetable fat spread. Sauté onions and garlic.*

2. Add minced lamb, tomatoes, mushrooms, parsley, tomato concentrate and stock to onions. Simmer 5-10 minutes. Season to taste.

3. Prepare cheese sauce. See page 121 in the sauce section.

3. Slice unpeeled aubergines lengthways. Sprinkle with salt. Leave for 30 minutes. Rinse. Drain on absorbent kitchen paper. Heat griddle pan or heavy based frying pan. Chargrill the aubergines, or place under hot grill for 2 minutes. Drain on absorbent kitchen paper.

4. Layer a baking dish with sliced aubergine, meat mixture and cheese sauce. Finish with a layer of aubergine and cover with cheese sauce. Sprinkle with parmesan cheese.

5. Bake in a preheated oven for 30-45 minutes or until the top is golden brown.

6. Serve hot or cold, with boiled potatoes and sliced green beans. Can be successfully reheated.

Light meal
Croque monsieur
Serves four

8 slices of white bread – crusts removed
8 slices gruyere or cheddar cheese
4 slices ham
2oz (50g) butter or vegetable fat spread

1. Take 4 slices of bread and cover with a slice of ham and a slice of cheese.

2. Cover with second slice of bread. Press gently together, and cut off crusts.

3. Melt butter or vegetable fat spread until foaming. Put sandwiches in pan. Sauté on both sides, until cheese has melted and bread is light brown. Put onto absorbent kitchen paper.

   or

   For weight watchers, toast the bread. Put ham on toast. Cover with grated cheese and place under h grill, until cheese is bubbling.

   Serve with a green salad.

*optional

Light meal
Croque monsieur
Serves four

Main meal
Vegetarian bolognese
Serves two

Pudding
Queen of puddings
Serves four

Day 12

Pudding
Queen of puddings
Serves four

1 pint (575ml) of milk (or low fat)
6oz (175g) breadcrumbs
2oz (50g) butter
2oz (50g) granulated sugar
2oz (50g) caster sugar
2 large eggs
grated rind of 2 lemons
4 tablespoons of raspberry jam

1. Preheat oven 180°C or 350°F or gas mark 4.

2. Heat milk until warm then add breadcrumbs,
   butter, lemon rind and granulated sugar.
   Leave for 30 minutes.

3. Separate eggs and stir yolks into milk and
   breadcrumb mixture.

4. Pour into buttered pie-dish and bake in a preheate
   oven for 30 minutes.

5. Remove from oven and reduce oven temperature
   to 150°C or 300°F or gas mark 2. Whip egg white
   until stiff then add 1oz (25g) of caster sugar.
   Whip again and fold in remaining 1oz (25g) suga

6. Spread jam on top of pudding and cover with
   meringue mixture.

7. Bake in oven for 20-25 minutes until meringue
   is set and golden brown. Watch carefully to ensur
   meringue does not burn.

Main meal
Vegetarian bolognese
Serves two

6oz (175g) brown lentils
4oz (100g) split peas
2 oz (50g) butter or vegetable fat spread
1 red onion – finely chopped
1 clove garlic – crushed*
4 cauliflower florets
2 carrots – peeled & cut very small
2 courgettes – thinly sliced
4 sticks celery – finely chopped
14oz (400g) can of tomatoes or 8oz (225g) cherry tomatoes
1 teaspoon dried oregano
2 tablespoons of chopped parsley
1 packet of whole-wheat spaghetti
generous amount of parmesan cheese – freshly grated
salt & freshly ground pepper

1. Soak brown lentils and split peas in boiling water for 1 hour.

2. Heat butter or vegetable fat spread until foaming. Sauté onion, garlic,* cauliflower, carrot, courgettes and celery. Simmer on low heat for 5 minutes. Stir in chopped tomatoes and oregano. Season to taste. Cover pan. Simmer for 5 minutes.

3. Add lentils and split peas and simmer a few more minutes.

4. Sprinkle with chopped parsley.

   Serve with wholewheat spaghetti and a green salad, accompanied by a bowl of parmesan cheese.

Light meal Macaroni & broccoli cheese Serves two

3oz (75g) macaroni
1oz (25g) butter or vegetable fat spread
1 oz (25g) plain flour
half a pint (275ml) milk (low fat or skimmed)
3oz (75g) grated low fat cheddar or red leicester
4oz (100g) broccoli florets
1 tablespoon breadcrumbs
salt & freshly ground pepper

1. Preheat oven 180°C or 350°F or gas mark 4.

2. Cook macaroni and put on one side.

3. For the white sauce melt butter or vegetable
   fat spread, add flour and blend in milk.
   Stir constantly until sauce boils and thickens.

4. Add grated cheese, stir again and season to taste.

5. Put broccoli in boiling water for 3-4 minutes.
   Drain. Put broccoli and macaroni in ovenproof di
   Cover with cheese sauce. Sprinkle with grated che
   and breadcrumbs. Cook in oven for 30 minutes o
   until cheese is bubbling and brown.

   Serve with a green salad.

**Light meal
Macaroni &
broccoli cheese
Serves two**

**Main meal
Warm chicken salad
Serves two**

**Pudding
Baked bananas
Serves two**

Day 13

Pudding
Baked bananas
Serves two

4 bananas – peeled & cut in two lengthways
2 tablespoons of brown sugar
1oz (25g) butter or vegetable fat spread
1 tablespoon lemon juice

1. Preheat oven 180°C or 350°F or gas mark 4.

2. Peel and slice the bananas. Put in shallow ovenproof dish.

3. Sprinkle with brown sugar and lemon juice. Dot with butter.

4. Put in a preheated oven for approximately 15 minutes.

   Serve with cream or crème fraiche.

Main meal
Warm chicken salad
Serves two

4 chicken breasts
2 tablespoons plain flour
1 packet of mixed salad leaves
6 florets of broccoli
1 packet of mange tout
1oz (25g) butter or vegetable fat spread
1 tin of baby sweet corn
1 tablespoon of balsamic vinegar or use 1 tablespoon of
white wine vinegar mixed with 1 teaspoon of brown sugar
1 teaspoon walnut oil
1 teaspoon soy sauce
2 tablespoons chopped chives
salt & freshly ground pepper

1. Cut chicken breasts into small pieces and roll in seasoned flour.

2. Wash and drain salad of all moisture and put in bowl.

3. Boil broccoli for 5 minutes. Drain.

4. Put mange tout in boiling water for 2 minutes. Drain.

5. Heat butter or vegetable fat spread until foaming and cook chicken pieces for 5 minutes. You can use a wok to prepare this dish. Instant noodles can be added to the chicken and heated through in the wok before serving. Add broccoli, mange tout and sweetcorn to chicken.

6. Add balsamic vinegar, walnut oil and soy sauce to chicken and season to taste.

7. Put warm chicken and vegetables on top of salad and sprinkle with chives.

Serve with tomato salad and noodles.

For those with nut allergies substitute walnut oil
for olive oil.

4

Light meal
Orange salad
with pinenuts
Serves two

ingredients
preparation

4 *large juicy oranges*
1 *head of endive – torn into small pieces*
bunch of watercress – trimmed & any stems removed
half a celeriac – peeled & thinly grated
6 *radishes – thinly sliced*
1 *red pepper – white membrane & seeds removed*
5oz (150g) *crème fraiche or natural yoghurt*
2oz (50g) *pinenuts*
salt & freshly ground pepper

instructions

1. Remove peel and pith from three of the oranges.
   Hold oranges over a bowl to catch the juice.
   Using a sharp knife cut orange segments from
   covering membrane. Be careful!

2. Mix together orange segments, endive, watercress
   celeriac, radishes and pepper.

3. Using rind zester, remove rind from remaining
   orange. Squeeze the juice from the orange. Mix
   together orange juice, orange rind, crème fraiche
   or yoghurt. Put in a sauceboat and season to taste

4. Sprinkle pinenuts over the salad.

   Serve with the orange dressing.

optional   4

**Light meal
Orange salad
with pinenuts
Serves two**

**Main meal
Lamb cutlets in
redcurrant sauce
Serves two**

**Pudding
Fruit salad
Serves two/four**

Day 14

Pudding
Fruit salad
Serves two/four

(SYRUP)
4oz (100g) caster sugar
quarter of a pint (150ml) water
juice & rind of 1 lemon
juice of 1 orange
2 or 3 tablespoons of dry white wine*
2 tablespoons of orange liqueur*

2 oranges
1 punnet strawberries – hulled & cut in half
1 mango – peeled & sliced
1 papaya – peeled, sliced & seeds removed
4 kiwi fruit – peeled & sliced
2 passion fruit – cut in half, scoop out seeds & juice
1 melon – use a melon baller to scoop out flesh
2 red skinned apples – thinly sliced but not peeled
8oz (225g) black seedless grapes

1. (SYRUP) Put 4oz (100g) sugar and 2 tablespoons water into a pan. Heat gently to dissolve sugar. Then boil until syrup begins to turn brown and harden. Add the rest of the water and boil to dissolve the caramel.

2. Remove from heat and allow to cool. Stir in lemon juice, orange juice, wine* and orange liqueur.* Put to one side.

3. Hold oranges over a bowl to catch any juice. Using a sharp knife remove skin and white pith. Cut orange segments out of their covering membrane. Be careful!

4. Hull strawberries and cut in half. Peel mango then slice off flesh and cut into cubes. Peel papaya, remove seeds and slice. Peel kiwi fruit and slice. Scoop flesh out of melon. Cut apples into four, remove pips and slice thinly. You can also vary the fruits used according to the seasons.

5. Combine the fruit, put in bowl and cover with syrup.

Main meal
Lamb cutlets in
redcurrant sauce
Serves two

2 lamb cutlets
2 sprigs fresh rosemary leaves
1 dessertspoon olive oil
1 tablespoon plain flour
quarter of a pint (150ml) of stock (use a stock cube)
2 large tablespoons of redcurrant jelly
quarter of a pint (150ml) red wine*
2 cloves garlic*
salt & freshly ground pepper

1. Pull green leaves off rosemary stalk. Place leaves
    in a cup and chop with kitchen scissors.

2. Heat oil in frying pan. Fry the cutlets for 4 minutes
    each side. The meat should be slightly pink.
    Remove from pan and keep warm.

3. Drain excess oil from frying pan. Sprinkle
    flour over juices in frying pan and blend in stock.
    Add jelly, chopped rosemary and wine if using.
    Season to taste and simmer for a couple of minutes.

4. Remove from heat and strain sauce into gravy-boat.

    Serve with mashed potato and garden peas.

5

Light meal
Toad in the hole
with parsnip purée
Serves two/four

1lb (450g) sausages
1oz (25g) butter or vegetable fat spread

(BATTER)
4oz (100g) plain flour
a pinch of salt
1 egg
half a pint (275ml) milk

(PARSNIP PURÉE)
1lb (450g) parsnips
2oz (50g) butter or vegetable fat spread
2 tablespoons cream or milk
chopped parsley
salt & freshly ground pepper

1. Preheat oven 190°C or 375°F or gas mark 5.

2. Sieve flour and salt in basin. Break egg into flour, and whisk in well.

2. Blend milk into flour, whisking until batter is thi and smooth. Leave to stand for 30 minutes.

3. Melt 1oz (25g) butter or vegetable fat spread in ovenproof dish. Prick sausages and put in ovenpro dish. Bake in a preheated oven for 15 minutes.

4. Remove sausages from the oven and increase temperature to 200°C or 400°F or gas mark 6, and pour the batter over the sausages. Return to the o and cook for about 30 minutes. Batter should rise and be golden brown. Serve with parsnip purée.

5. (PARSNIP PURÉE) Peel and slice parsnips. Boil for 5-10 minutes until tender. Put parsnips in food processor and reduce to a purée. Beat in cream an a knob of butter or vegetable fat spread. Season to taste. Sprinkle with chopped parsley.

*optional

Light meal
Toad in the hole
with parsnip purée
Serves two/four

Main meal
Fish fillets
with vegetables
Serves two

Pudding
Apple meringue
Serves two/four

Day 15

Pudding
Apple meringue
Serves two/four

1lb (450g) cooking apples
1 tablespoon water
2oz (50g) caster sugar
2 egg yolks
grated rind & juice of 1 lemon

(MERINGUE)
2 egg whites
4oz (100g) caster sugar

1. Preheat oven 170°C or 325°F or gas mark 3.

2. Peel and core apples. Cut into slices, put into a pan and add water and sugar.

3. Cover and simmer at low heat for 5 minutes. Leave to cool.

4. Add egg yolks, lemon juice and rind to apples. Pour into ovenproof dish.

5. (MERINGUE) Whisk egg whites until stiff, then whisk in 2 tablespoons of sugar. Fold in remainder of sugar with metal spoon. Pile meringue on top of apple.

6. Bake in a preheated oven for 20 minutes, or until meringue is golden. Watch carefully to ensure that the meringue does not burn.

   Serve with créme fraiche.

Main meal
Fish fillets
with vegetables
Serves two

2oz (50g) butter or vegetable fat spread
6oz (175g) baby carrots – scrubbed & trimmed
1 fennel bulb – thinly sliced
2 courgettes – thinly sliced
grated rind of 1 lemon
sprigs of parsley
2 × 6oz (175g) skinned cod, salmon or halibut fillets
quarter of a pint (150ml) white wine
slices of lemon
1 tablespoon chopped parsley
salt & freshly ground pepper

1. Melt butter or vegetable fat spread in covered pan. Add carrots, fennel, courgettes, lemon rind and parsley.

2. Arrange fish fillets on top of vegetables.

3. Season to taste. Add white wine. Cover and simmer on low heat for 5-10 minutes. Do not overcook.

4. Lift fish fillets onto a warm serving dish. Surround with the vegetables.

5. Strain wine juices and pour over fish.

   Serve garnished with lemon slices and sprigs of parsley accompanied with new potatoes.

6

Light meal
Chicken risotto
Serves two

2 red peppers
4oz (100g) butter or vegetable fat spread
1 red onion – peeled & sliced
8oz (225g) clean risotto rice
half a pint (275ml) chicken stock (use more if not using
wine)
1 clove of garlic – squeezed*
quarter of a pint (150ml) red wine*
4oz (100g) sliced mushrooms
6oz (175g) cooked chicken – cut in bite sized pieces
2oz (50g) freshly grated parmesan cheese
salt & freshly ground pepper

1. Grill peppers under hot grill until skin blisters
   and turns black. Put peppers in plastic bag to coo
   The skin will come off once cold.

2. Heat 2oz (50g) butter or vegetable fat spread. Sau
   onion on low heat. Add risotto rice and sauté for
   minutes. Turn rice with fork to check if the rice i
   absorbing the liquid. Risotto rice should not be
   soggy. Add stock and garlic and wine and bring t
   boil. Lower heat and simmer until liquid has bee
   absorbed into rice. This can take up to 20 minute
   Stir well and add extra stock if necessary.

3. Sauté mushrooms in remaining butter or vegetab
   fat spread. Drain off excess moisture.

4. Take peppers out of bag and skin. Remove white
   membrane and then slice.

5. Mix chicken, peppers, mushrooms and buttery ju
   with the rice. Re-heat and season to taste. Sprink
   with parmesan cheese

   Serve with a green salad and crusty bread.

*optional   4

Light meal
Chicken risotto
Serves two

Main meal
Vegetarian lasagne
Serves two

Pudding
Poached pears
in red wine
Serves four

Day 16

Pudding
Poached pears
in red wine
Serves four

4 large dessert pears
5oz (150g) caster sugar
quarter of a pint (150ml) red wine
quarter of a pint (150ml) water
1 teaspoon arrowroot

1. Peel pears leaving stalks on.

2. Put sugar, water and wine in saucepan.
   Heat gently until sugar is dissolved.
   Bring to the boil and simmer for 2 minutes.

3. Put pears upright in syrup. Cover and simmer
   for 15 minutes, or until the pears are soft.

4. Transfer pears to serving dish.

5. Mix arrowroot with a teaspoon of water and add
   to syrup. Bring to the boil and simmer for 1 min
   until syrup is clear. Leave to cool and once cold p
   over pears.

   Serve hot or cold with shortbread biscuits.

Main meal
Vegetarian lasagne
Serves two

12oz (325g) pre-cooked lasagne

(CHEESE & SPINACH SAUCE)
3oz (75g) butter or vegetable fat spread
1 red onion – peeled & sliced
3oz (75g) flour
1 teaspoon dried mustard powder
1 pint (575ml) milk
2 tablespoons of Dijon mustard
6oz (175g) grated cheddar cheese
1lb (450g) spinach – cooked fresh or frozen
half a teaspoon of nutmeg

(TOMATO SAUCE)
2oz (50g) butter or vegetable fat spread
1 carrot
1 stick celery
1 onion
8oz (225g) cherry tomatoes
1 clove garlic*
2 teaspoons sugar
half a pint (275ml) red wine*
quarter of a pint (150ml) stock
salt & freshly ground pepper

1. Preheat oven to 180°C or 350°F or gas mark 4.

2. (TOMATO SAUCE) Heat butter or vegetable fat spread.

3. Sauté carrot, celery and onion for a couple of minutes. Add tomatoes. Season to taste and add garlic* and sugar. Pour in red wine, or stock. Simmer for 15 minutes. Purée in food processor.

4. (CHEESE & SPINACH SAUCE) Heat butter or vegetable fat spread and sauté onion a couple of minutes. Add flour and mustard powder. Blend in milk. Bring to boiling point and stir until sauce is smooth. Add Dijon mustard, cheese and spinach. Season to taste, adding nutmeg.

5. Layer an ovenproof dish with lasagne, tomato sauce and cheese and spinach sauce. Finish with tomato sauce. Sprinkle with grated cheese.

6. Bake in preheated oven for 30-40 minutes, or until the sauce is bubbling and brown on top.

7

Light meal
Scrambled eggs
Serves two

1 slice of brown bread
2oz (50g) butter or vegetable fat spread
2 eggs
salt & freshly ground pepper
watercress tips or smoked salmon to garnish

1. Toast the bread. Melt butter or vegetable fat sprea
   and pour over beaten eggs. Mix in well and seasor
   to taste.

2. Pour mixture into saucepan and cook on low heat,
   turning with a wooden spoon. Once cooked, eggs
   should be moist not dry. Do not overcook.

3. Place scrambled eggs on buttered toast and decora
   with watercress or strips of smoked salmon.

   *If using organic eggs, add 2 teaspoons cold water
   when beating. This gives a lighter texture.*

Light meal
Scrambled eggs
Serves two

Main meal
Hamburgers with
mushroom sauce
Serves four

Pudding
Fruit crumble
Serves four

Day 17

Pudding
Fruit crumble
Serves four

4 apples – peeled & sliced
4 pears – peeled & sliced
1 banana – peeled & sliced
3 tablespoons brown sugar
3 tablespoons raspberry jam
8oz (225g) flour
4oz (100g) butter or vegetable fat spread
4oz (100g) caster sugar

1. Preheat oven 180°C or 350°F or gas mark 4.

2. Peel and slice fruit, add brown sugar and simmer for 5 minutes in saucepan.

3. Crumble butter, flour and sugar together until mixture resembles breadcrumbs.

4. Put fruit in ovenproof dish and cover with crumb mixture.

5. Bake in a preheated oven for 20 minutes or until golden brown.

    Serve with whipped cream.

Main meal
Hamburgers with mushroom sauce
Serves four

2 finely chopped onions
1oz (25g) butter or vegetable fat spread
1lb (450g) finely minced lean steak – purée in processor
1 teaspoon English mustard
1 beaten egg
salt & freshly ground pepper
a pinch of flour

(MUSHROOM SAUCE)
2 tablespoons white wine*
1lb (450g) baby mushrooms – cleaned & sliced
1 teaspoon lemon juice
1 clove garlic*
2 small cartons of sour cream

1. Sauté onions in butter or vegetable fat spread until soft.

2. Mix mince, onions, mustard and beaten egg and season to taste. Shape into small rounds and roll in seasoned flour. Leave to rest.

3. Melt butter or vegetable fat spread in pan and fry hamburgers on both sides until brown and crisp.

4. (MUSHROOM SAUCE) Put white wine* in saucepan and bring to the boil. Add mushrooms, lemon juice and garlic.* Remove from heat and stir in sour cream. Season to taste and put in sauceboat.

Serve with new potatoes and cauliflower florets.

8

Light meal
Spinach pie
Serves two

1lb (450g) spinach – fresh or frozen
1lb (450g) cream cheese (or low fat)
half a pint (275ml) sour cream
4 eggs – separated
quarter of a pint (150ml) milk (or low fat)
8oz (225g) filo pastry – in wafer thin sheets
2oz (50g) butter or vegetable fat spread – melted
salt & freshly ground pepper
nutmeg to taste

1. Preheat oven 180°C or 350°F or gas mark 4.

2. Wash spinach and strip off leaves. Sprinkle leaves with salt and leave for 30 minutes. Wash and drain spinach thoroughly.

3. Mix together cream cheese, sour cream, egg yolks and milk. Season to taste. Whisk egg whites and fold into cheese mixture.

4. Lay filo pastry sheets flat and brush with melted butter or vegetable fat spread.

5. Line ovenproof dish with a layer of filo pastry, followed by a layer of cheese mixture, followed by a layer of spinach mixture. Sprinkle a little nutmeg over each layer of spinach. Repeat until the dish is full. Finish with a layer of filo pastry.

6. Press the pie into the dish and brush with melted butter or vegetable fat spread.

7. Bake in a preheated oven for 30-35 minutes until the spinach pie has risen and is golden brown.

   Cut into squares and serve hot or cold with a green salad.

Light meal
Spinach pie
Serves two

Main meal
Quick chicken bake
Serves two

Pudding
Bread & butter
pudding
Serves two

Day 18

Pudding
Bread & butter puddin
Serves two

6 *slices white bread with crusts removed*
2oz (50g) unsalted butter
2oz (50g) sultanas
2oz (50g) caster sugar
2 large eggs
1 pint (575ml) milk (or low fat)
nutmeg to taste

1. Preheat oven 170°C or 325°F or gas mark 3.

2. Spread bread with butter and cut each slice into four pieces.

3. Place bread butter side down in buttered ovenproof dish.

4. Add sultanas and 1oz of sugar.

5. Heat the milk until just warm and add beaten egg. Pour over buttered bread.

6. Sprinkle with nutmeg and remaining sugar. Leave for 30 minutes.

7. Bake in a preheated oven for 30 minutes until top crisp and golden.

Main meal
Quick chicken bake
Serves two

4 chicken thighs
1 × 14oz (400g) tin of cream of mushroom soup
3 spring onions
pinch of curry powder
juice of half a lemon

1. Preheat oven 180°C or 350°F or gas mark 4.

2. Put chicken in ovenproof dish.

3. Chop spring onions and sprinkle over chicken.

4. Mix together the mushroom soup, lemon juice and curry powder, pour over chicken and cover with silver foil.

5. Bake in moderate oven for 40 minutes.

   Serve with a green salad and pasta. You can buy packets of prepared mixed salad from your local supermarket. For variety add cherry tomatoes, mustard and cress, radishes, celery, etc.

9

Light meal
Eggs mornay
Serves two

4 potatoes
2oz (50g) butter or vegetable fat spread
half a pint (275ml) milk (or low fat)
4 hard boiled eggs – chopped

(CHEESE SAUCE)
1oz (25g) butter or vegetable fat spread
1oz (25g) flour
half a pint (275ml) milk (or low fat)
4oz (100g) grated cheese
salt & freshly ground pepper

1. Preheat oven 200°C or 400°F or gas mark 6.

2. Peel potatoes and boil for 10-15 minutes. Drain a mash potatoes, adding 2oz (50g) butter or vegetabl fat spread and 1 tablespoon of milk. Beat potatoes until smooth, seasoning to taste. Put potato in an ovenproof dish.

3. (CHEESE SAUCE) Melt butter or vegetable fat spre over low heat and stir in flour. Blend in milk, brin to boil, reduce heat and stir until smooth.

4. Add 2oz (50g) grated cheese and stir well. Remove from heat and mix in hard boiled eggs.

5. Make a nest in the mashed potatoes and pour cheese sauce into centre. Sprinkle with 2oz (50g) grated cheese. and place in a preheated oven and bake for 15 minutes until hot and bubbling.

Serve with carrots.

**Light meal
Eggs mornay
Serves two**

**Main meal
Fish cakes
Serves two**

**Pudding
Baked apples
Serves two**

Day 19

Pudding
Baked apples
Serves two

2 large cooking apples
1oz (25g) stoned dates
1oz (25g) raisins
2oz (50g) soft brown sugar
half a teaspoon ground cinnamon
2 tablespoons cider

1. Preheat oven 180°C or 350°F or gas mark 4.

2. Remove core from apples, using an apple corer.

3. Chop dates and mix with raisins, sugar and cinnamon. Press mixture into centre of apples.

4. Place apples in ovenproof dish with cider.

5. Bake in a preheated oven for 40 minutes.

   Serve hot with cream.

Main meal
Fish cakes
Serves two

2 × 6oz (175g) cod or haddock fillets
half a pint (275ml) milk (or low fat)
2oz (50g) butter or vegetable fat spread
1 onion – peeled & sliced
4oz (100g) cooked mashed potato
4oz (100g) white bread
1 beaten egg
1 tablespoon chopped parsley
salt & freshly ground pepper

1. Skin fish and remove bones. Put fish in saucepan, cover with milk and bring to the boil. Remove saucepan from heat and leave fish to cool in milk.

2. Heat 1oz (25g) butter or vegetable fat spread and sauté onion until soft. Mash potatoes using a little milk from the fish. Keep potatoes fairly dry.

3. Put bread in food processor and process to crumbs.

4. Remove fish from the milk and flake into small pieces. Mix together fish, mashed potato, onion, egg and parsley. Shape mixture into small cakes 2 inches in diameter and roll in the breadcrumbs. Put in a cool place.

5. Heat remaining butter or vegetable fat and sauté fish cakes for a minute or two on each side until reheated and crisp and golden.

   Serve with carrots.

Light meal
Sardine savoury
with grilled tomatoes
Serves one

1 × 4oz (100g) tin of sardines
1 teaspoon lemon juice
1 tablespoon chopped parsley
slice of bread — toasted
1oz (25g) grated cheddar cheese
2 large tomatoes
1 tablespoon of sugar
1 tablespoon of breadcrumbs
salt & freshly ground pepper

1. Remove sardines from can. Discard bones. Mash sardines. Add lemon juice and chopped parsley.

2. Spread mixture on toasted bread. Sprinkle with grated cheese. Put under hot grill, until cheese bubbles.

3. Cut tomatoes in half and put in an ovenproof dish Sprinkle with a mixture of sugar and breadcrumb Season to taste. Place under hot grill for 4-5 minu

Light meal
Sardine savoury
with grilled tomatoes
Serves one

Main meal
Baked gammon
with honey glaze
Serves four

Pudding
Citrus fool
Serves four

Day 20

Pudding
Citrus fool
Serves four

1 packet of sponge fingers
4 oranges
2 lemons
1 pint (575ml) double cream
*1-2 tablespoons icing sugar**

1. Line a medium sized soufflé dish with sponge fing
   round the sides, and on the base.

2. Grate the peel of 4 oranges and 1 lemon.

3. Squeeze the juice of 4 oranges and 1 lemon and
   put the juice and peel together in bowl.

4. Lightly whip cream and fold into juice and peel.
   Sweeten to taste with sieved icing sugar.*

5. Pour orange and lemon cream over sponge fingers
   Chill in fridge for 2 hours.

Main meal
Baked gammon
with honey glaze
Serves four

2lb (1kg) piece of gammon
2 tablespoons honey
2oz (50g) soft brown sugar
juice of 1 lemon
2 tablespoons of Dijon mustard

1. Place gammon skin side down in saucepan of cold water. Bring water to the boil and boil for 4 minutes. Remove from heat and pour away cooking water. Refill saucepan with fresh water, and replace the gammon. Bring to the boil again, lower heat and simmer for 30 minutes per LB (450g) of gammon. Leave gammon to cool in cooking liquid.

2. Preheat oven 200°C or 400°F or gas mark 6.

3. Once cold remove gammon and strip off rind using a sharp knife. Score the fat in a criss-cross pattern.

4. Mix honey, sugar, lemon juice and mustard and spread over fat.

5. Bake gammon in a preheated oven for 20-30 minutes until gammon is reheated and honey glaze has caramelised. Baste during baking.

   Serve hot or cold with boiled potatoes and broad beans.

Light meal
Watercress, potato & bacon salad
Serves two

1lb (450g) small new potatoes
8 rashers of streaky bacon
olive oil or sunflower oil
1 tablespoon white wine vinegar
1 bunch watercress – trimmed of thick stalks
salt and freshly ground pepper

1. Boil potatoes 5-10 minutes. Drain.

2. Fry bacon in its own fat until crisp.
   Remove from pan and cut into small pieces.

3. Add oil, vinegar, salt and freshly ground pepper
   to pan and stir well to blend in bacon juices.

4. Add potatoes and bacon to juices in pan and stir
   well to coat with dressing. Place on a serving dish
   and decorate with watercress leaves.

*optional

**Light meal
Watercress, potato
& bacon salad
Serves two**

**Main meal
Steak & kidney pie
Serves four**

**Pudding
Raspberry jelly
Serves two**

Day 21

Pudding
Raspberry jelly
Serves two

1 packet of raspberry flavoured jelly
1 × 8oz (225g) punnet of raspberries
quarter of a pint (150ml) double cream
2 ramekin dishes

1. Follow instructions on jelly packet. (Homemade fresh fruit jelly is better, but takes longer to make. Pour half of the jelly and the raspberries into the ramekin dishes.

2. Place in a refrigerator until set.

3. Once jelly is beginning to set pour over remaining jelly – this is to ensure jellies have flat bottoms when turned out.

4. Return to the refrigerator and chill until set.

5. Turn jellies out onto individual plates.

   Serve with cream and decorate with reserved raspberries.

   If you want a taste of fresh fruit in the jelly, substitute puréed raspberries for some of the water required to make the jelly.

Main meal
Steak & kidney pie
Serves four

2oz (50g) butter or vegetable fat spread
1 large onion – peeled & sliced
1lb (450g) lean stewing steak – cut into small pieces
8oz (225g) ox kidney – remove white membrane & slice
1 tablespoon Worcester sauce
1 teaspoon tomato sauce
half a pint (275ml) beef stock
1oz (25g) flour
1 packet frozen short-crust pastry
1 egg – beaten
1 clove garlic – peeled & squeezed*
pinch of mixed herbs*
salt & freshly ground pepper

1. Preheat oven 200°C or 400°F or gas mark 6.

2. Heat butter or vegetable fat spread in saucepan and sauté onion until soft.

3. Add stewing steak and kidney and cook until browned. Add Worcester sauce, tomato sauce and stock. Bring to the boil, lower heat and simmer for 90 minutes. Leave to cool.

4. Roll out pastry on a floured work surface until sightly larger than the pie dish.

5. Put an egg cup into the middle of the pie dish and spoon in meat. Moisten the rim of the pie dish and press strips of pastry round the edge.

6. Cover with pastry lid, and seal the edges with a fork. Cut an air vent above the egg cup and let the steam escape. Brush the pastry with a beaten egg and bake in a preheated oven for 30 minutes until pastry is crisp and brown.

   Serve with mashed potatoes and peas.

Light meal
Small omelette
Serves one

*ingredients
preparation*

2 eggs
1oz (25g) butter or vegetable fat spread
salt & freshly ground pepper
1 tablespoon chopped parsley

(CHEESE)
2 tablespoons parmesan cheese or grated cheddar cheese
1 tablespoon chives

(CHICKEN)
2oz (50g) chicken – cooked & diced

(SPINACH)
warm 2 tablespoons of cooked, well-drained spinach
in 1oz (25g) butter or vegetable fat spread. Add one
crushed garlic clove* and season to taste.

instructions

1. Break 2 eggs into a bowl. Season well to taste.

2. Put butter or vegetable fat spread in omelette pan. Heat over medium flame until butter begins to fo – do not burn. Beat eggs and pour melted butter vegetable fat spread into egg mixture. Whisk and pour eggs into hot omelette pan.

3. As eggs begin to set, stir with fork in order to distribute mixture. Eggs should remain moist and soft.

4. As eggs are beginning to set, add one of the abov flavourings. Remove from heat.

5. Slide omelette towards panhandle. Once a third of the omelette has slid towards the handle, fold i towards the centre. Raise handle of pan and slide opposite edge of omelette a third of the way away from the handle. Fold remainder of omelette towa the centre.

6. Slide omelette onto serving dish.

7. Garnish with chopped parsley.

Serve with brown toast.

*optional

**Light meal
Small omelette
Serves one**

**Main meal
Coq au vin
Serves four**

**Pudding
Caribbean brulée
Serves four**

Day 22

Pudding
Caribbean brulée
Serves four

1 pint (575ml) yoghurt (or low fat)
half a pint (275ml) of whipping cream
4 tablespoons brown sugar
1 kiwi fruit
2 small bananas
1 small pineapple – skinned & chopped
1 mango – peeled & sliced

1. Lightly whip cream and fold yoghurt into cream.

2. Cut up fruit and fold into yoghurt and cream.
   Pour into serving bowl.

3. Sprinkle a thick layer of brown sugar over the crea
   Chill for a couple of hours.

   Serve with shortbread biscuits.

Main meal
Coq au vin
Serves four

1 chicken (jointed) or 8 individual pieces
1 Spanish onion – peeled & sliced
20 small onions – peeled
10z (275g) streaky bacon
1 large tablespoon brandy
three quarters of a bottle red wine
2oz (50g) butter or vegetable fat spread
1 bouquet garni
8oz (225g) button mushrooms
2 cloves garlic*
2oz (50g) plain flour
1 tablespoon chopped parsley
salt & freshly ground pepper

1. Preheat oven 190°C or 375°F or gas mark 5.

2. Dip chicken pieces in seasoned flour.

3. Put small onions in boiling water for 4 minutes. Drain. The skin should then peel off easily.

4. Peel and chop Spanish onion and dice bacon. Heat butter vegetable fat spread and cook onion and bacon until onion is transparent and bacon is crisp. Remove from pan and put to one side.

5. Saute chicken pieces in butter vegetable fat spread until brown on each side.

6. Gently heat brandy in saucepan. Remove brandy from heat and ignite. A flame will spring up and quickly subside. Pour brandy over chicken pieces.

7. Gently warm red wine and pour over chicken. Add spanish onion, bacon, bouquet garni, garlic, small onions and seasonings.

8. Cover and cook in a preheated oven for 1 hour. Allow to cool and degrease the sauce.

9. Add whole button mushrooms to the coq au vin before reheating. Reheat in moderate oven for half and hour. Sprinkle with chopped parsley.

Serve with anna potatoes and haricot vert.

This dish is better made the day before, the flavour improves.

3

Light meal
Cauliflower
& potato bake
Serves two/four

1 lb (450g) potatoes
1 small cauliflower – broken into florets
half a teaspoon of nutmeg
1 clove of garlic – squeezed*
1 pint (575ml) fresh single cream
4oz (100g) cheddar cheese
salt & freshly ground pepper

1. Preheat oven 180°C or 350°F or gas mark 4.

2. Boil potatoes for 2 minutes, drain and cut into sli

3. Plunge cauliflower in boiling water for 2 minutes

4. Layer potatoes and cauliflower in lightly buttered ovenproof dish. Season to taste.

5. Stir nutmeg and garlic* into cream and pour over potatoes and cauliflower. Sprinkle with grate cheese. Bake in a preheated oven for 30-40 minut until vegetables are tender and cheese is bubbling

   Serve with a stick of French bread.

*optional

Light meal
Cauliflower
& potato bake
Serves two/four

Main meal
Grilled salmon fillets
with Danish cucumber
Serves two

Pudding
Pancakes
Serves four

Day 23

Pudding Pancakes Serves four

8oz (225g) plain flour
half a teaspoon salt
2 eggs
1 pint (575ml) milk
2oz (50g) butter or vegetable fat spread
2oz (50g) caster sugar
lemon juice
lemon wedges to serve

1. Sieve flour and salt into basin and make well in centre and break in eggs.

2. Add milk and draw in eggs and flour using a wire whisk. Whisk thoroughly then leave to rest for 30 minutes.

3. Melt 1oz (25g) of butter or vegetable fat spread in frying pan or omelette pan. Heat until fat is just smoking. Pour fat away and wipe pan with kitchen paper. This is to prevent pancakes sticking to the pan.

4. Melt 1oz (25g) of butter or vegetable fat spread in pan. Heat until just smoking. Pour in enough bat to coat the bottom of the pan, making sure it runs evenly over base of pan.

5. Move pan over heat until pancake is set and brown underneath. Loosen sides with broad bladed knife or spatula. Turn and cook on other side.

6. Turn out onto greaseproof paper sprinkled with sugar.

7. Roll pancake and sprinkle with sugar and lemon juice. Keep warm while cooking the rest of the pancakes.

Serve with lemon slices.

Main meal
Grilled salmon fillets
with Danish cucumber
Serves two

2 large salmon fillets
4 tablespoons butter or vegetable fat spread – melted
2oz (50g) butter or vegetable fat spread
2 tablespoons chopped parsley
lemon juice

(DANISH CUCUMBER)
1 cucumber – cut into thin slices
salt & sugar
salt & freshly ground pepper

1. Preheat grill on high.

2. Place salmon fillets on silver foil in baking tin. Brush with melted butter or vegetable fat spread. Grill 3-5 minutes each side.

3. (PARSLEY BUTTER) mix softened butter, with chopped parsley and 1 teaspoon of lemon juice. Season to taste. Wrap in cling film. This will keep for several days in the fridge.

4. (DANISH CUCUMBER) Slice cucumber very thin and put in bowl. Sprinkle with 1 tablespoon of salt and 1 tablespoon of sugar. Leave for 1 hour. Drain away liquid and rinse cucumber in cold water. Drain thoroughly.

Serve with new potatoes sprinkled with chopped mint and a dish of Danish cucumber.

Light meal
Potted shrimps
Serves two/four

8oz (225g) small brown shrimps – rinsed
6oz (175g) unsalted butter
1 lemon – sliced
2 slices of brown bread
2-4 ramekin dishes

1. Divide shrimps among 2-4 ramekin dishes.

2. Heated unsalted butter until foaming. Strain through a sieve lined with muslin and pour over shrimps in the ramekin dishes. Leave to set.

3. Turn potted shrimps out onto a plate, and decorate with lettuce leaves and slices of lemon.

   Serve with brown bread. lightly buttered and cut into triangles.

*optional

**Light meal
Potted shrimps
Serves two/four**

**Main meal
Lamb salad &
mint dressing
Serves two**

**Pudding
Trifle
Serves two**

Day 24

Pudding
Trifle
Serves two

1 packet of trifle sponges
3 tablespoons raspberry jam
3 egg yolks
2 teaspoons cornflour
1oz (25g) caster sugar
three quarters of a pint (475ml) milk
quarter of a pint (150ml) double cream
3 tablespoons sherry
2 small bananas
blanched almonds & glace cherries to garnish

1. Cut the trifle sponges in half. Spread with jam and put in glass bowl.

2. Beat egg yolks, pour the sherry over the cornflour and sugar and stir until smooth.

3. Heat milk and pour over egg mixture, stirring well

4. Return mixture to pan and heat until mixture coat back of the spoon. Cool.

5. Slice bananas and add to trifle sponges and pour custard over bananas and leave to set.

6. Spread a layer of lightly whipped cream on top an decorate with blanched almonds and glace cherries

   You can use custard powder if you do not want to make real custard.

Main meal
Lamb salad &
mint dressing
Serves two

half a cucumber
1 tablespoon salt
1 tablespoon caster sugar
1 cos lettuce
8 thin slices of cold roast lamb
1 small carton of natural yoghurt
1 teaspoon clear honey
2 teaspoons finely chopped mint
1 sliced red pepper – seeds & membrane removed
1 sliced green pepper – seeds & membrane removed
2 ripe pears – peeled & sliced
4 spring onions – thinly sliced
garnish with sprigs of mint

1. Peel and thinly slice cucumber and put in bowl. Sprinkle with 1 tablespoon salt and 1 tablespoon sugar – leave for 1 hour. Drain off liquid and pat with absorbent kitchen paper.

2. Tear lettuce into small pieces.

3. Carve thin slices of lamb.

4. Mix together yoghurt, honey, and chopped mint.

5. Put lettuce, cucumber, peppers, pears and spring onions on plate. Lay slices of lamb over salad and drizzle dressing over the salad.

5 Light meal
Grilled sardines
Serves one

redients
preparation

2 fresh sardines – gutted
olive oil
juice of 1 lemon
1 squeezed garlic clove*
salt & freshly ground pepper

tructions

1. Rub sardines with kitchen paper to remove loose scales.

2. Brush with olive oil. Put squeezed garlic inside the sardines.

3. Place on silver foil in grill pan and grill for 3-4 minutes each side.

4. Place on heated serving dish and season with freshly ground pepper. Sprinkle with lemon juice.

5. Serve with a soft roll and a mixed salad.

*optional

**Light meal
Grilled sardines
Serves one**

**Main meal
Baked chicken
& orange
Serves four**

**Pudding
Fruit meringue
Serves two/four**

Day 25

Pudding
Fruit meringue
Serves two/four

1 tin of black cherries – pitted
3oz (75g) frozen summer fruits
1 packet of trifle sponges
quarter of a pint (150ml) double cream
2 egg whites
4 oz (100g) caster sugar

1. Layer soufflé dish with trifle sponges.

2. Drain the moisture from summer fruits and black cherries onto the sponges.

3. Place the fruit on the top. Whip cream and spread over fruit.

4. Whisk egg whites until stiff and add 2oz (50g) caster sugar and whisk until stiff and shiny. Fold in remaining 2oz (50g) of caster sugar.

5. Spread meringue on top of whipped cream. Place under a hot grill for a few minutes. Take care – as it browns very quickly.

Main meal
Baked chicken
& orange
Serves four

1 small chicken (jointed) or 4 chicken breasts (skinless)
8oz (225g) dried breadcrumbs
grated rind & juice of 2 oranges
2 eggs
4oz (100g) butter or vegetable fat spread
salt & freshly ground pepper
1 orange – sliced
watercress

1. Preheat oven 190°C or 375°F or gas mark 5.

2. Mix breadcrumbs and orange rind, season to taste and put in shallow dish.

3. Beat eggs and orange juice and pour into a shallow dish.

4. Dip chicken pieces in egg and orange juice mixture and then in breadcrumb mixture. Pat on well.

5. Heat butter or vegetable fat spread in ovenproof dish. Put chicken in dish and bake for 30-40 minutes until chicken is crisp and brown.

6. Add extra breadcrumbs during cooking.

7. Decorate with slices of orange and watercress.

   Serve with mashed potatoes and courgettes.

Light meal
Steamed or baked eg
Serves one

1 small ramekin dish
1 egg
1 teaspoon butter or vegetable fat spread
1 teaspoon cream
salt or freshly ground pepper

(A COMBINATION OF ANY OF
THE FOLLOWING FLAVOURINGS)
a pinch of parsley – chopped
a pinch of tarragon – chopped
a pinch of chervil – chopped
a pinch of marjoram – chopped
a pinch of rosemary – chopped

ham – finely chopped
chicken – finely chopped
fried crisp bacon – finely chopped
shrimps
cooked mushrooms – diced

1. Put flavouring in bottom of ramekin dish.
   Break egg onto flavouring.

2. Put butter and cream on top of egg and season
   to taste.

3. (TO STEAM) Place ramekin dish in a covered pan
   with 1 inch of boiling water on bottom of pan.
   Steam for 5-10 minutes.
   (TO BAKE) Place ramekin dish in baking tin
   with 1 inch of water in the bottom of tin. Bake c
   180°C or 350°F or gas mark 4 for 5-10 minutes.

   Serve with lightly buttered brown bread.

Light meal
Steamed or baked egg
Serves one

Main meal
Vegetable curry
Serves two

Pudding
Blackberry &
apple crumble
Serves two

Day 26

Pudding Blackberry & apple crumble Serves two

3oz (75g) butter or vegetable fat spread
6oz (175g) plain flour
3oz (75g) brown sugar
1lb (450g) cooking apples
8oz (225g) blackberries
3oz (75g) granulated sugar

1. Preheat oven 180°C or 350°F or gas mark 4.

2. Rub butter or vegetable fat spread into flour using tips of fingers until the mixture resembles breadcrumbs.

3. Stir in brown sugar.

4. Peel, core and slice apples. Mix with blackberries and granulated sugar and place in ovenproof dish.

5. Cover with crumble mixture and bake in a prehea oven for 40 minutes until golden brown.

Main meal
Vegetable curry
Serves two

2oz (50g) butter or vegetable fat spread
1 red onion – peeled & sliced
1 teaspoon curry powder
1 teaspoon ground coriander
1 teaspoon ground cumin
half a teaspoon chilli powder
half a teaspoon ground turmeric
1 garlic clove*
6 tomatoes – skinned & sliced
1 small cauliflower – cut into florets
2 potatoes – peeled & sliced
3 carrots – peeled & sliced
2 courgettes – sliced
1 tin of sweetcorn
1 small head of broccoli – cut in florets
1 green pepper –sliced
1 yellow pepper – sliced
1 large teacup of cooked rice
1 carton plain yoghurt (or low fat)
salt & freshly ground pepper

1. Heat butter or vegetable fat spread in pan. Sauté onion and spices.

2. Skin tomatoes by leaving in boiling water for 1 minute. Leave to cool and peel skin off.

3. Add garlic* tomatoes, cauliflower, potatoes, carrots, courgettes, (or other vegetables can be used in making the curry) sweet corn, broccoli and peppers to onions and spices. Simmer for 10-15 minutes until vegetables are tender.

4. Remove from heat and season to taste.

   Serve on a bed of rice, accompanied by poppadoms, mango chutney and plain yoghurt.

7

Light meal
A salad for cold days
Serves two

3 eggs – hard boiled & sliced
1 eating apple – cored & chopped
1 head of celery – chopped
1 cooked beetroot – peeled & sliced
4oz (100g) of thinly sliced raw or cooked celeriac
6 radishes
1 punnet of mustard & cress
a few leaves from the top of the celery
half a teaspoon English mustard
1 teaspoon sugar
2 tablespoons fresh single cream
2 tablespoons white wine vinegar
4 tablespoons olive oil
salt & freshly ground pepper
chopped parsley

1. Combine apple, celery, beetroot, radishes, celeriac cress and eggs and put in salad bowl.

2. Mix English mustard, sugar, cream, olive oil and vinegar and season to taste.

3. Decorate salad with chopped parsley and celery leaves. Pour dressing over salad and serve at once.

   Serve with French bread.

Light meal
A salad for cold days
Serves two

Main meal
Sole Veronique
Serves two

Pudding
Rice pudding
Serves two/four

Day 27

Pudding
Rice pudding
Serves two/four

1 pint (575ml) of milk (or low fat)
3oz (75g) pudding rice
2-3oz (50-75g) sugar
ground cinnamon
nutmeg

(ONE OF THE FOLLOWING FLAVOURINGS)
1 teaspoon vanilla essence
2 teaspoons lemon or orange rind
1oz (25g) dried fruit

1. Preheat oven 180°C or 350°F or gas mark 4.

2. Heat milk until warm then sprinkle pudding rice
   into the milk. Stir to prevent lumps forming and
   simmer for 10 minutes. Add sugar and flavouring
   Also add extra milk if required.

3. Put into a dish and bake in a preheated oven for
   10 minutes.

4. Sprinkle ground cinnamon or nutmeg on top
   of pudding.

Main meal
Sole Veronique
Serves two

2 large or 4 small fillets of Dover or lemon sole
1 onion – peeled & sliced
2 tablespoons of parsley
1oz (25g) butter or vegetable fat spread
1 tablespoon flour
quarter of a pint (150ml) single cream
4oz (100g) green seedless grapes – cut in half
half teaspoon dried tarragon
a pinch of ground nutmeg
1 tablespoon grated parmesan cheese
quarter of a pint (150ml) water
or quarter of a pint (150ml) dry white wine*
salt & freshly ground pepper

1. Put fish with skin removed., onion and parsley in a covered pan. Add enough wine or water to cover. Bring to the boil and remove pan from heat.

2. Leave fish to cool in stock – this keeps it moist.

3. Put fish in ovenproof dish. Boil fish stock until liquid is reduced by half. Strain into bowl.

4. Melt butter or vegetable fat spread. Add flour and blend in fish stock. Stir until sauce is smooth. Cool and add cream, grapes, tarragon, nutmeg and pepper.

5. Pour sauce over fish. Sprinkle with grated parmesan and brown under a hot grill.

6. Serve with new potatoes and green beans.

   Alternatively Dover sole can be painted with melted butter seasoned with freshly ground pepper and placed under hot grill for 5 minutes. Serve with a green salad and half a lemon. Simple but delicious!

8

Light meal
French toast
Serves one

1 egg
2 or 3 tablespoons of milk
2 slices of bread
2oz (50g) butter or vegetable fat spread
4oz (100g) grated cheddar cheese*
2 teaspoons pickle*
salt & freshly ground pepper*

1. Beat together egg and milk. Pour into a shallow c

2. Remove crusts from bread. Cut each slice into tw
   and soak bread in egg and milk mixture.

3. Melt butter or vegetable fat spread until foaming
   Fry french toast for 2 minutes on each side until
   golden brown.

   or

1. Mix cheese and pickle. Spread over French toast.
   Place under hot grill until cheese is bubbling.

   Serve with a salad and sliced tomatoes.

**Light meal
French toast
Serves one**

**Main meal
Roast pork in red wine
Serves four**

**Pudding
Apple tart
Serves one**

Day 28

Pudding
Apple tart
Serves one

frozen puff pastry
2 dessert apples
1oz (25g) caster sugar
1 beaten egg
1 tablespoon of warm apricot jam

1. Preheat oven 200°C or 400°F or gas mark 6.

2. Thaw pastry and roll out on a floured board. Using a large teacup cut a circle 5 inches across and 1 inch thick. Use a sharp knife to trace an inner circle 1 inch from edge of pastry. Do not cut through pastry.

3. Peel, core and slice apples. Arrange in overlapping circles coming to within 1 inch of edge of pastry.

4. Sprinkle with caster sugar. Brush pastry rim with beaten egg.

5. Bake in a preheated oven for 20 minutes.

6. Gently heat 1 tablespoon of apricot jam in a saucepan.

7. Cool and glaze apples with warm apricot jam.

Main meal
Roast pork in red wine
Serves four

2lb (1kg) boned loin of pork
3 red onions – peeled & sliced
4oz (100g) butter or vegetable fat spread
1 tablespoon chopped, fresh rosemary
half a pint (275ml) white wine vinegar
2 tablespoons brown sugar
1 small wineglass of red wine* or stock
salt & freshly ground pepper

1. Preheat oven 220°C or 425°F or gas mark 7.

2. Remove the rind and fat from the pork loin.
    Season the meat and seal on cast iron griddle or
    heavy based frying pan.

3. Melt butter or vegetable fat spread in roasting tin.
    Put pork, onions and rosemary in tin. Pour a quarter
    of a pint (150ML) of white wine vinegar mixed with
    1 tablespoon of brown sugar over pork. Baste well.

4. Roast in preheated oven. Pork should be roasted
    30 minutes per lb (450g) of weight and an extra 30
    minutes as well.

5. Add remaining quarter of a pint (150ML) white wine
    vinegar and 1 tablespoon brown sugar to the pork 5
    minutes before the end of the cooking time.

6. Remove pork from oven and leave to rest for
    5-10 minutes.

7. Drain fat from roasting tin. Add red wine, or stock
    to the pan juices. Stir well and season to taste.

8. Carve pork in thin slices. Put in serving dish and
    add some red onions, rosemary and pan juices.

    Serve with carrots and mashed potatoes.

Miscellaneous
Additional meals

Beef Stroganoff
Serves two

gredients
preparation

1lb (450g) rump or fillet steak
1 heaped tablespoon flour
1 onion – finely chopped
2oz (50g) butter or vegetable fat spread
2 tablespoons brandy*
8oz (225g) button mushrooms
quarter of pint (150ml) sour cream
salt & freshly ground pepper

structions

1. Trim meat. Cut into strips and roll in seasoned flc

2. Chop onion. Sauté in butter or vegetable fat sprea
   Add meat and simmer for 5-10 minutes.

3. Heat brandy* in saucepan. Remove from heat
   and ignite. A flame will briefly flare up. Pour bra
   over meat.

4. Add mushrooms and sour cream. Do not boil.

   Serve with boiled potatoes and red cabbage.

*optional

Carbonnade of beef
Serves two/four

2lbs (1kg) lean stewing steak
1 tablespoon flour
2 tablespoons butter or vegetable fat spread
4 onions – sliced
half a pint (275ml) guinness
salt & freshly ground pepper

1. Preheat oven 180°C or 350°F or gas mark 4.

2. Cut steak into small pieces. Roll in seasoned flour.

3. Heat butter or vegetable fat spread in casserole dish. Brown meat for 2 minutes and remove from casserole.

4. Sauté onions. Return meat to casserole. Season to taste. Add guinness, cover and cook in preheated oven for 2 hours.

   Serve with mashed potatoes and broad beans.

Chicken Marengo
Serves four

ingredients
preparation

1 chicken – or 4-8 pieces of chicken
1oz (25g) butter or vegetable fat spread
3 tablespoons olive oil or sunflower oil
1 onion – peeled & sliced
1oz (25g) flour
half a pint (275ml) white wine*
half a pint (275ml) stock
2 tablespoons tomato purée
1 bouquet garni
1lb (450g) button mushrooms
1 tablespoon chopped parsley
salt & freshly ground pepper

instructions

1. Preheat oven 180°C or 350°F or gas mark 4.

2. Skin chicken and joint into eight pieces.

3. Dip in seasoned flour.

4. Heat butter or vegetable fat spread and oil. Sauté chicken pieces and remove to casserole.

5. Sauté onion, adding more butter or vegetable fat spread if necessary. Do not burn. If pan is dirty wipe with kitchen paper and start again with fresh butter or vegetable fat spread.

6. Add onion, tomato purée and bouquet garni to the chicken. Season to taste and cover with white wine or stock. Cook in a preheated oven for one hour.

7. Cool and degrease sauce.

8. Add raw sliced mushrooms to the cold chicken marengo. Reheat in medium oven for 30 minutes.

   Serve on bed of rice and sprinkle with chopped parsley.

   It is always better to make a dish like this the day before, it improves the flavour. Remember to take off any congealed fat.

*optional

7

Cutlets of lamb
with tomato sauce
Serves two

4 cutlets of best end of lamb
1oz (25g) butter or vegetable fat spread
4 large tomatoes

(SAUCE)
1.5lb (700g) cherry tomatoes
1 teaspoon of chopped tarragon
1 tablespoon brown sugar
salt & freshly ground pepper

1. Season cutlets. Fry or grill. Meat should be just pink inside. Reserve juices from meat.

2. (SAUCE) Add cherry tomatoes and tarragon to pan juices. Simmer until tomatoes are soft, stirring all the time. Add sugar. Season to taste.

3. Strain sauce through a sieve.

4. Sprinkle 4 large tomatoes with brown sugar. Season to taste and place under hot grill until cooked and sugar bubbling.

5. Place cutlets and tomatoes on serving dish.

   Serve sauce separately with mashed potatoes.

Farmhouse paté
Serves six

ingredients
preparation

1lb (450g) minced chicken liver
half a lb (225g) minced pork
half a lb (225g) sausage meat
3 eggs – beaten
half a pint (275ml) cream
1 tablespoon chopped parsley
1 glass of brandy or white wine* or use stock
2 cloves garlic*
salt & freshly ground pepper

instructions

1. Preheat oven 180°C or 350°F or gas mark 4.

1. Put liver, pork and sausage meat into food process
   Process until smooth. Add beaten eggs, cream,
   parsley, brandy* white wine* or stock and garlic.
   Process again and season to taste.

2. Pour into lined buttered rectangular tin. Cover w
   silver foil. Put paté tin into a baking tin filled wi
   1 inch of water. Cook in preheated oven for 2 hou
   or until the meat leaves the side of the tin.

3. Cool and remove fat. Cover with silver foil and al
   to cool, refrigerate for 24 hours.

4. Turn out onto serving plate.

   Cut in slices and serve with a green salad and son
   warm bread.

Fillet of Beef Wellington Serves four

1 × 2lb (1kg) fillet of beef
1 4oz (100g) tin of meat pate
half a lb (225g) mushrooms
1 onion – sliced
2oz (50g) butter or vegetable fat spread
1 tablespoon dry sherry
1 packet of puff pastry
freshly ground pepper

1. Preheat oven 220°C or 425°F or gas mark 7.

2. Pepper meat and dot with butter. Roast for 5 minutes each side in hot oven. Leave to cool.

3. Melt butter or vegetable fat spread and sauté onion. Add mushrooms and sherry. Add the pate and mix well together.

4. Spread mushroom mixture over cold meat.

5. Roll out pastry and place meat in the centre. Wrap pastry round meat folding it under at the ends. Decorate the pastry with thin strips of pastry in a criss-cross pattern. Moisten strips of pastry with water to hold in place. Brush pastry with egg yolk. Place in baking dish on silver foil.

6. Cook in a preheated oven for 30 minutes until pastry is risen and golden brown.

   Serve with duchess potatoes and haricot beans.

   This is a very extravagant dish – plain roast fillet of beef is just as delicious.

Fricassee of chicken
Serves four

8oz (225g) breadcrumbs
1 poached chicken
3 tablespoons Worcester sauce
1 tablespoon soy sauce
1 teaspoon dried mustard
2 teaspoons Dijon mustard
a pinch of cayenne pepper
2oz (50g) butter or vegetable fat spread
1 tablespoon plain flour
half a pint (275ml) milk (low fat)
2 rashers bacon – diced
3 tomatoes – peeled & sliced
6 sticks celery – sliced
2 tablespoons chopped parsley
salt & freshly ground pepper
parsley or watercress to garnish

1. Preheat oven 180°C or 350°F or gas mark 4.

2. Put bread into a food processor and reduce to crumbs. Toast crumbs in preheated oven for 20 minutes until light brown.

3. Put chicken in large saucepan and cover with cold water. Bring to the boil. Lower heat and simmer for 50 minutes. Leave chicken to cool in stock. Strip flesh off chicken and cut into small pieces.

4. Marinate chicken pieces in soy, Worcester sauce, mustard and cayenne pepper for 20 minutes minimum.

5. Melt 1oz (25g) butter or vegetable fat spread in saucepan. Add flour and blend in milk stirring all the time. Stir until sauce boils and thickens.

6. Melt 1oz (25g) butter or vegetable fat spread and fry bacon. Add peeled tomatoes and sliced celery. Add bacon, tomato and celery to chicken. Cover with white sauce. Season to taste.

8. Garnish with chopped parsley and watercress. Or cover with toasted breadcrumbs and knobs of butter or vegetable fat spread. Reheat in oven on 190°C or 375°F or gas mark 5 for 10-15 minutes until breadcrumbs are crisp and brown.

Serve with mashed potatoes and courgettes.

Grilled chicken
Serves four

4 pieces of chicken
1oz (25g) butter or vegetable fat spread
3 tablespoons mild Dijon mustard
1 teaspoon dried mustard
1 large tablespoon brown sugar
1 teaspoon paprika pepper
juice & rind of 1 lemon
2oz (50g) butter or vegetable fat spread
salt & freshly ground pepper

1. Preheat oven 190°C or 375°F or gas mark 5.

2. Melt 1oz (25g) butter or vegetable fat spread and mix with mustard, sugar and paprika.

3. Put 1oz (25g) butter or vegetable fat spread in baking tin.

4. Spread the butter and mustard mixture over one side of the chicken. Season to taste. Put in baking tin and bake for 10 minutes.

5. Turn chicken over. Spread with remaining mustard mixture. Sprinkle with paprika, sugar and lemon juice. Season to taste. Bake a further 10 minutes.

6. Put chicken in ovenproof dish. Drain fat from baking tin, reserving pan juices. Brown chicken under a hot grill for a couple of minutes. Do not burn.

7. Pour pan juices over chicken and garnish with watercress.

   Serve with new potatoes and tomato salad.

Grilled trout with bacon & almonds
Serves one

1 trout – cleaned
juice of half a lemon
salt & freshly ground pepper
1 tablespoon plain flour
1oz (25g) slivered almonds
1oz (25g) butter or vegetable fat spread
2 rashers of streaky bacon
1 tablespoon chopped parsley or dill

1. Preheat grill to high. Line grill pan with silver-fo

2. Cut three slashes down the sides of the trout, being extra careful with the bones.

3. Sprinkle with lemon juice, salt and pepper. Dust with flour, place trout on silver-foil and grill for 4 minutes each side.

4. Gently sauté almonds in butter or vegetable fat spread. Remove from pan and put on one side.

5. Dice bacon and fry for 3 minutes until crisp. Add almonds, parsley or dill and stir together.

6. Place trout in serving dish. Cover with bacon and almond mixture.

   Serve with boiled potatoes and broccoli florets, garnished with lemon slices.

Kedgeree
Serves two

8oz (225g) rice
4 hard boiled eggs
3oz (75g) butter or vegetable fat spread
10oz (275g) cooked smoked haddock or salmon – flaked
quarter of a pint (150ml) cream*
salt & freshly ground pepper

1. Cook rice. Rinse rice in sieve under running water. (This will get rid of the starch).

2. Take four hard-boiled eggs and cut in quarters.

3. Melt butter or vegetable fat spread. Add fish and eggs. Sauté on a low heat.

4. Season to taste – but not too much salt! Mix rice, fish and eggs. Reheat over a low heat.

5. Stir in cream if using or butter or vegetable fat spread.

6. Put kedgeree in serving dish. Sprinkle with chopped parsley.

   Serve with crisp green salad.

Leg of lamb with a parsley crust
Serves four

Ingredients
preparation

1 × 2lb (1kg) leg of lamb
4 rashers of bacon
8oz (225g) fresh breadcrumbs
2 tablespoons chopped parsley
2oz (50g) butter or vegetable fat spread
1 clove of garlic*
1 tablespoon plain flour
quarter of a pint (150ml) lambstock
1 glass sherry
mint sauce or recurrant jelly
gravy granules to thicken

Instructions

1. Preheat oven 190-200°C or 375-400°F or gas mark 5-6.

2. Weigh lamb to calculate cooking time. (See page 8 at the beginning of the book for cooking times and charts).

3. Heat butter or vegetable fat spread in roasting tin. Cover lamb with bacon. Roast lamb in preheated oven.

4. Mix breadcrumbs, parsley and crushed garlic.* Half an hour before end of cooking spread mixture over lamb. Return to oven for 20 minutes.

5. Put lamb on heated serving dish. (GRAVY) Drain fat from roasting tin. Add flour to pan juices and stir. Blend in stock or water. Add a glass of sherry and gravy granules. Stir until gravy is smooth. Season to taste and strain into a sauce-boat.

Serve with steamed potatoes and green beans.

*optional

Lamb stew
Serves four

2lbs (1.1kg) boned shoulder or breast of lamb
2 tablespoons flour
2oz (50g) butter or vegetable fat spread
1 Spanish onion – sliced
1 pint (575ml) stock (stock cube)
4 small turnips – peeled & diced
4 tablespoons tomato concentrate
1 large tablespoon soft brown sugar
2 cloves garlic*
salt & freshly ground pepper
12 small white onions – skins removed
4oz (100g) bacon
12 small potatoes – peeled & quartered
4oz (100g) peas
2 tablespoons chopped parsley

1. Cut lamb in small pieces. Roll in seasoned flour.
   Heat butter or vegetable fat spread. Sauté onion in
   a casserole dish. Add lamb and stir over a low heat
   until brown. Add stock, turnips, tomato concentrate,
   brown sugar and garlic.* Season to taste.

2. Simmer on a low heat for 1 hour. (Simmering can
   also be done in a slow oven.)

3. Leave overnight in the refrigerator. Skim fat off
   top of stew.

4. Preheat oven 170°C or 325°F or gas mark 3.

5. Boil small onions for 2 minutes. Drain and peel
   off their skin.

6. Fry bacon and add onions, potatoes and bacon to
   the casserole dish.

7. Cook in a preheated oven for 40 minutes. Cool and
   skim fat off top of stew.

8. Reheat in low oven for 30 minutes. Sprinkle with
   some chopped parsley. This dish is best made the
   day before.

   Serve with parsnip and fennel salad. See page 116
   of the salad section.

Pork in a white wine sauce Serves two

1lb (450g) tenderloin of pork – thinly sliced
10z (25g) butter or vegetable fat spread
1 onion – finely chopped
quarter of a pint (150ml) white wine
2 cloves of garlic – squeezed*
6oz (175g) mange tout
4 tablespoons single cream
1 tablespoon chopped parsley
salt & freshly ground pepper

1. Heat butter or vegetable fat spread until foaming
   Sauté pork and onion for 3-4 minutes.

2. Add white wine and garlic.* Simmer for 3 minu

3. Add mange tout and simmer for 5 minutes.
   Season to taste.

4. Remove from heat. Add cream* and sprinkle
   with parsley.

   Both the garlic and the cream are optional. A be
   egg can be substituted for cream. Do not add the
   to a hot mixture, as it will scramble.

   Serve with new potatoes or pasta.

*optional

Potato pie
Serves one

4oz (100g) cold mashed potato
1 egg
2oz (50g) butter or vegetable fat spread – melted
2 tablespoons milk (low fat)
2oz (50g) grated cheddar cheese
1 tablespoon chopped chives
2oz (50g) finely chopped ham or bacon
salt & freshly ground pepper

1. Preheat oven 180°C or 350°F or gas mark 4.

2. Beat egg into smooth mashed potato. Add butter or vegetable fat spread and milk. Season to taste.

3. Place in an ovenproof dish. Sprinkle with cheddar cheese and bake in a preheated oven until risen and golden brown. Fold 2oz (50g) chopped ham or bacon* into potato mixture.

4. Sprinkle with chives and serve.

Outback stew
Serves four

ngredients
preparation

2lb (1kg) lean stewing steak

4 onions

6 carrots

3 parsnips

2 tablespoons Worcester sauce

2 tablespoons tomato ketchup

2 tablespoons white wine or balsamic vinegar

2 tablespoons brown sugar

2 tablespoons flour

salt & freshly ground pepper

stock to cover – use stock cube

instructions

1. Preheat oven 180°C or 350°F or gas mark 4.

2. Cut steak into small pieces. Roll in seasoned flour

3. Peel and slice onions, carrots and parsnips.

4. Take a casserole dish and layer with meat and vegetables. Finish with a layer of vegetables. Add enough water or stock to cover the meat.

5. Add vinegar, brown sugar, tomato ketchup and Worcester sauce. Stir and season to taste.

6. Cover tightly and cook over a low heat for 2-2.5 hours.

   Serve with baked potatoes and green cabbage.

*optional

Oxtail stew
Serves four

2lb (1kg) oxtail
1 × 6oz (175g) tin chopped tomatoes
1 large tin of guinness
half a pint (275ml) beef stock (use stock cube)
2oz (50g) butter or vegetable fat spread
2 onions
1 teaspoon thyme
2 tablespoons redcurrant jelly
pinch of nutmeg
gravy granules to thicken
salt & freshly ground pepper
2 tablespoons freshly chopped parsley

1. Preheat oven 180°C or 350°F or gas mark 4.

2. Trim oxtail and removing fat. Heat butter or
    vegetable fat spread in thick-bottomed pan
    until brown. Add sliced onions and oxtail and
    sauté until golden.

3. Purée tomatoes in liquidizer. Add to oxtail together
    with the tin of guinness, thyme and stock. Bring to
    the boil. Remove from heat, cover and put in
    preheated oven for 2.5 hours. Check during cooking.

4. Remove from heat. Cool and refrigerate overnight.
    Skim off fat.

5. The following day skim off any more fat.
    Add redcurrant jelly and thicken with gravy
    granules. Reheat in medium oven for 1 hour.

6. Season to taste and sprinkle with a handful of freshly
    chopped parsley.

    Serve with creamy mashed potatoes and green
    cabbage.

    *Oxtail should be cooked until the meat just leaves the
    bone – overcooking ruins the flavour. Raw meat should
    be brightly coloured & carry a reasonable amount of creamy
    white fat.*

Roast beef & Yorkshire pudding Serves two/four

2lb (1kg) joint of beef
butter or vegetable fat spread
olive oil or sunflower oil
1 jar of horseradish sauce

(YORKSHIRE PUDDING)
8oz (225g) plain flour
2 eggs
1 pint milk
half a teaspoon salt
1 tablespoon olive oil

1. Weigh meat to calculate cooking time. (Please refer to cooking times on page 8. Do not overcook

2. Preheat oven to 220°C or 425°F or gas mark 7. Put mixture of butter or vegetable fat spread and oil in roasting tin. Heat to smoking and season beef on all sides.

3. Put beef in oven for 10-15 minutes. Reduce heat 190°C or 375°F or gas mark 5 and continue cooki Baste every 30 minutes.

4. When cooked the beef juices should have some blood. There should be a rich brown sediment of juices at the bottom of the roasting tin. Drain off fat, leaving rich brown sediment in roasting ti (GRAVY) Sprinkle flour over pan juices. Stir well and blend in stock or water, stirring until sauce is smooth. Gravy granules can be added at this stage. Season to taste. Strain into sauceboa

5. (YORKSHIRE PUDDING) Preheat oven on 200°C or 400°F or gas mark 6. Sift flour and salt into a basin. Make a well in the centre. Break eggs into flour. Gradually add milk, working flour in from sides of bowl. Whisk and leave the batter to stand for 30 minutes.

6. Put oil or fat from roasting tin into Yorkshire pudding tin. Heat until smoking. Pour in batter and cook in a preheated oven for an hour until ri Yorkshire pudding should be light, crisp and bro

7. Reduce heat. Keep puddings warm until ready to serve.

   Serve with roast potatoes and glazed carrots.

*optional

9

Roast brace of grouse or pheasant Serves two

1 brace of grouse (2 birds)

or

1 pheasant – plucked & prepared for roasting
3 rashers of bacon
2oz (50g) butter or vegetable fat spread
flour
2 pieces of toast

1. Preheat oven to 200°C or 400°F or gas mark 6.

2. Insert a piece of butter or vegetable fat spread inside the cavity of each bird.

3. Cover the breast of the birds with bacon.

4. Roast in preheated oven for 30 minutes. Baste during cooking.

5. After 20-25 minutes remove bacon. Dredge with flour. Baste and return to oven for 10 minutes until skin is brown and crisp.

6. Toast the bread. Place toast under pheasant or grouse for last 15 minutes of cooking time. Toast will absorb cooking juices and should remain crisp.

7. Serve birds on slices of toast accompanied by bread sauce, gravy and fried breadcrumbs. Garnish with watercress.

   Serve with brussels sprouts and mashed potatoes.

Roast lamb
Serves two/four

2lb (1kg) leg of lamb
salt & freshly ground pepper
2oz (50g) butter or vegetable fat spread
clove of garlic*
mint sauce or redcurrant jelly
1 tablespoon plain flour
quarter of a pint (150ml) lamb stock
8 medium sized roasting potatoes

1. Weigh the lamb to calculate cooking time. (Pleas refer to cooking times on page 8. Do not overcook

2. Preheat oven to 220°C or 425°F or gas mark 7. Heat butter or vegetable fat spread in roasting tir

3. Season lamb with salt and freshly ground pepper. Rub with garlic clove.

4. Roast lamb for 20 minutes in hot oven. Reduce h to 190°C or 375°F or gas mark 5, juices should ru slightly pink and skin should be crisp and brown Do not overcook.

5. (GRAVY) Drain fat from roasting tin. Sprinkle flour over pan juices. Stir well. Blend in a quarter a pint (150ML) stock or water and stir until smoo Strain into sauceboat.

6. (ROAST POTATOES) Peel potatoes and cut in half. Put in boiling water for 4 minutes. Drain and dip potatoes in seasoned flour. Put in roasting tin wit the lamb. Baste with hot fat and cook for 1 hour until crisp and brown.

   Serve with small brussels sprouts and mint sauce redcurrant jelly.

*optional

Roast pork
Serves two/four

2lb (1kg) boned pork loin – with rind & fat removed
3 red onions – peeled & sliced
4oz (100g) butter or vegetable fat spread
1 tablespoon fresh rosemary – chopped
half a pint (275ml) white wine vinegar
4 tablespoons brown sugar
1 small wine glass of red wine*
salt & freshly ground pepper

1. Preheat oven to 220°C or 425°F or gas mark 7.

2. Season the meat. Seal on cast iron griddle or heavy based frying pan.

3. Melt butter or vegetable fat spread in roasting tin. Put pork, onions and rosemary in tin. Pour a quarter of a pint (150ML) white wine vinegar mixed with 2 tablespoons of brown sugar over pork. Baste pork.

4. Roast in preheated oven. Pork should be roasted for 30 minutes per LB (450g) of weight and 30 minutes over.

5. Add remaining quarter of a pint (150ML) of white wine vinegar and 2 tablespoons brown sugar 5 minutes before the end of the cooking time.

6. Remove pork from oven and leave to rest.

7. Drain fat from roasting tin. Add red wine, or stock to the pan juices. Stir well. Season to taste.

8. Carve pork in thin slices. Put in serving dish. Cover with red onions, rosemary and pan juices.

Serve with carrots and mashed potatoes.

Stuffed marrow
Serves two/four

1 marrow
1 lb (450g) cooked minced meat – beef or lamb
4oz (100g) breadcrumbs (reduce to crumbs in food proces
1 large egg
1 bunch chopped parsley
4 eating apples
8oz (225g) mushrooms
4 grated carrots
salt & freshly ground pepper

1. Preheat oven 180°C or 350°F or gas mark 4.

2. Wash marrow, slice off top and reserve. Hollow ou
   centre of marrow. Do not pierce skin.

3. Mix meat, breadcrumbs, egg, parsley, apples
   and mushrooms.

4. Line baking dish with silver foil.

5. Fill marrow with meat mixture. Replace marrow t
   Put in baking dish.

6. Bake in a moderate oven for 45 minutes until
   marrow is soft. Cut marrow in slices.

   Serve with boiled potatoes and a tomato salad.

*optional

Swedish meatballs
Serves four

1 onion – peeled & chopped
4oz (100g) fresh breadcrumbs
1lb (450g) minced beef or lamb
1 beaten egg
half a teaspoon nutmeg
1 tablespoon tomato sauce
1lb (450g) cherry tomatoes
1 tablespoon brown sugar
2oz (50g) butter or vegetable fat spread
salt & freshly ground pepper

1. Preheat oven 180°C or 350°F or gas mark 4.

2. Sauté onion until golden. Put bread into food processor and process into breadcrumbs.

3. Put mince in food processor and process until smooth. Add beaten egg, nutmeg and onion. Season to taste.

4. Shape mince into balls. Roll meatballs in breadcrumbs. Leave to chill. This will make approximately 12-16.

5. Purée cherry tomatoes. Add brown sugar. Season to taste.

6. Sauté meatballs in 2oz (50g) foaming butter or vegetable fat spread for 4 minutes each side. Put in ovenproof dish. Cover with tomato sauce. Bake in a preheated oven for 15 minutes.

   Serve with mashed potatoes and runner beans.

Welsh rarebit
Serves one

1oz (25g) butter or vegetable fat spread
2oz (50g) grated gruyere cheese
2oz (50g) grated cheddar cheese
1 teaspoon of milk, beer & whisky to moisten
1 egg
1 slice of toast – lightly buttered
1 teaspoon Dijon mustard
salt & freshly ground pepper
*a pinch of cayenne pepper**

1. Preheat grill to a high temperature.

2. Melt butter or vegetable fat spread in a saucepan. Add cheese, milk, beer, or whisky. Stir until sauce is smooth and cheese melted. Allow to cool. Add beaten egg and Dijon mustard. Season to taste.

3. Spread cheese mixture on toast. Place toast on silver-foil under hot grill, and grill until cheese mixture has risen and is light brown.

4. Serve with sliced tomatoes.

*optional

Miscellaneous
Cakes & puddings

Fruitcake

3 eggs
6oz (175g) butter or vegetable fat spread
6oz (175g) sugar
8oz (225g) plain flour
quarter of a teaspoon salt
1 teaspoon baking powder
1 teaspoon cinnamon
quarter of a teaspoon ground or grated nutmeg
grated rind of 1 lemon
6oz (175g) currants
3oz (75g) stoned chopped raisins
4oz (100g) sultanas
2oz (50g) chopped mixed peel
2oz (50g) chopped almonds
4 tablespoons brandy or whisky*
milk
2oz (50g) blanched almonds

1. Preheat oven 180°C or 350°F or gas mark 4.

2. Line a 7 inch cake-tin with greaseproof paper.

3. Cream butter and sugar. Add eggs, one at a time. If they look like curdling, add flour to stabilise.

4. Stir in brandy or whisky.*

5. Sieve flour, baking powder and salt and add to the mixture along with the fruit and chopped almonds

6. Mix well adding a little milk if mixture is too dry

7. Place mixture in cake tin.

8. Press the almonds on top of the cake.

9. Bake in moderate oven for 45 minutes. Reduce the heat to 150°C or 300°F or gas mark 2 and bake for hour. Cover with greaseproof paper if top becomes too brown.

   To test if cooked insert a skewer, if the skewer comes out clean the cake is cooked.

Ice cream bombe

1 large block of good quality vanilla ice cream

(FILLING)
half a pint (275ml) double cream
2oz (50g) icing sugar
2 egg whites
vanilla essence
8oz (225g) mixed glace fruits – marinated in rum*
2 pudding bowls – one small & one large

1. Take two pudding bowls. On small and one large. Line the large bowl with vanilla ice cream. Put the small bowl inside the large and press it against the ice cream. Put into the freezer to set.

2. Remove inner bowl and fill cavity with glace fruit filling. To move inner bowl ease hot knife, (heated under boiling water), between bowl and ice cream.

3. (FILLING) Whip cream and add 1oz (25g) sugar. Whisk egg whites until stiff. Fold in the remaining sugar.

4. Fold cream and egg whites together. Add vanilla essence and chopped fruits. Spoon filling into the centre of the ice cream. Level the top. Cover and freeze.

5. To serve dip bowl in boiling water. Turn out onto a serving dish.

   Serve surrounded with marinated glace fruits.*

   For a chocolate coated ice cream bombe. Melt 8oz (225g) plain chocolate. Pour chocolate around inside of a large pudding bowl. Put in ice cream once chocolate has hardened. To turn out, place pudding basin in boiling water to soften chocolate. Invert onto serving plate.

Jam sponge

8oz (225g) self-raising flour
8oz (225g) sugar
3 eggs

1. Preheat oven 190° C or 375°F or gas mark 5.

2. Beat eggs. Add flour and sugar. Mix all together with wire whisk.

3. Grease and flour baking tins.

4. Bake sponge in preheated oven for 15-20 minutes or until springy to the touch. Turn out onto wire rack to cool.

5. Fill with jam and whipped cream.

6. Pass icing sugar through a sieve and dust over the sponge.

   Best eaten on the day of baking.

Lemon shortbread

8oz (225g) unsalted butter
6oz (175g) plain flour
6oz (175g) cornflour
4oz (100g) icing sugar
1 egg yolk
grated rind of 2 small lemons
enough lemon juice to bind

1. Preheat oven 180°C or 350°F or gas mark 4.

2. Mix all ingredients in food processor until they become a spongy dough.

3. Using palm of hand, gently roll dough on floured board. Cut into rounds using a biscuit cutter.

4. Bake in preheated oven for 15-20 minutes.

Makes about 20 pieces of shortbread.

Scones

8oz (225g) self raising flour
2oz (50g) butter or vegetable fat spread
1oz (25g) sugar
quarter of a pint (150ml) milk (or low fat)

1. Preheat oven 200°C or 400°F or gas mark 6.

2. Sift flour and sugar into bowl. Rub in butter or vegetable fat spread until mixture resembles breadcrumbs.

3. Add milk by degrees. Stir with blade of knife.

4. Handle gently. Knead until mixture becomes a soft dough. Turn onto floured board. Roll out and cut into rounds.

5. Bake in a preheated oven for 10 minutes, or until risen. This should make about 12 scones. Delicious with clotted cream and raspberry jam.

Miscellaneous
Christmas

Roast turkey

(MEAT)

1 fresh turkey
2lb (1kg) chipolata sausages
1lb (450g) bacon

(HERB FORCEMEAT)

8oz(225g) breadcrumbs
4oz (100g) shredded suet
2oz (50g) melted butter or vegetable fat spread
1 tablespoon chopped parsley
1 teaspoon dried mixed herbs
1 large teaspoon of grated nutmeg
grated rind & juice of 1 lemon
2 eggs – beaten
salt & freshly ground pepper

1. Mix all ingredients together.

(SAUSAGE MEAT STUFFING)

2lbs (1kg) sausagemeat
turkey liver – washed & sliced
4oz (100g) white breadcrumbs
2 tablespoons chopped parsley
2 teaspoons dried mixed herbs
1 teaspoon grated nutmeg
1 teaspoon ground mace
2 eggs – beaten
salt & freshly ground pepper

1. Slice liver and mix with sausage-meat, breadcrum
   & herbs. Season to taste. Stir in beaten eggs.

(BREAD SAUCE)

1 pint milk
1 large onion – chopped
4oz (100g) white breadcrumbs
3 whole cloves
2 bay leaves
2 tablespoons butter
3 tablespoons single cream*
salt & freshly ground pepper

1. Put milk in saucepan with onion and spices
   and bring to the boil. Leave to infuse and cool.
   Strain milk and stir in breadcrumbs and butter
   and season to taste. (Bread sauce can be made in
   advance. Cover with silver foil to keep moist).

*optional

1. Preheat oven to 220°C or 425°F or gas mark 7 and melt some fat in the roasting tin. Calculate cooking time using chart on page 7.

2. Rinse the turkey inside and out, and wipe with a clean damp cloth. Stuff the neck with HERB FORCEMEAT and stuff the SAUSAGE MEAT STUFFING inside body cavity.

3. Season the turkey with salt and pepper. Put bacon over the breast.

5. Place the turkey and giblets in roasting tin and roast for 15-20 minutes. Lower heat to 180°C or 350°F or gas mark 4. Cover with foil and continue roasting.

6. Separate the chipolatas. Prick with a fork. Put in roasting tin for 30 minutes before end of cooking time.

7. Remove bacon 30 minutes before turkey comes out of oven. Baste breast with hot fat.

8. Once turkey is cooked juices should run clear and show no sign of pink. Put turkey and chipolatas on serving dish and put giblets to one side.

   (GRAVY) Drain fat from roasting tin into heatproof container. Sprinkle flour over pan juices and stir using a wooden spoon. Add 1 and a half pints (575-850ML) of water. The giblets can be boiled up and the stock used to make the gravy. Add 1 glass of wine and 2 tablespoons of redcurrant jelly. Season to taste. Strain gravy into sauce boat.

   As an approximate guide one 12lb turkey serves 6-8 people. If your turkey is smaller please adjust recipes accordingly. Forcemeat & stuffing can be ordered from the butcher. They may even stuff the turkey for you.

Christmas vegetables

(POTATOES)
2lbs (1kg) potatoes
flour
butter or vegetable fat spread

1. Peel potatoes and cut in half.

2. Boil for 5-10 minutes – the smaller the potato, the less the cooking time.

3. Drain and pat dry. Sprinkle with seasoned flour and put into hot fat in roasting tin. Baste and cook for 1 hour in a moderate oven, or until brown and crisp.

(BRUSSELS SPROUTS WITH CHESTNUT & HAM)
2lbs (1kg) brussels sprouts
12-16 cooked chestnuts (fresh or tinned)
3oz (75g) chopped ham
4 tablespoons single cream
salt & freshly ground pepper

1. Remove outer leaves of brussels sprouts and slice off woody base.

2. Boil 5-7 minutes. Do not overcook and then drain.

   Cut chestnuts in half, and put in casserole together with brussels sprouts and ham. (Can be prepared in advance to this stage.)

3. Reheat. Add cream and season to taste.

(CARROTS & LEEKS)
1lb (450g) carrots
12oz (325g) leeks
2oz (50g) butter or vegetable fat spread
quarter of a pint (150ml) cider
4 tablespoons single cream
salt & freshly ground pepper

1. Top, tail, scrape and slice carrots. Wash, trim and slice leeks.

2. Heat butter or vegetable fat spread in saucepan. Add carrots, leeks and cider. Simmer on low heat for 10-15 minutes. Stir to prevent vegetables sticking to bottom of pan or becoming brown. Season to taste. (Can be prepared in advance to this stage.)

*optional

3. Reheat then remove vegetables with slatted spoon. Keep warm. Boil cooking liquid for a couple of minutes. Remove from heat. Add cream and pour over vegetables.

(PEAS WITH BACON & ONION)
1.5lb (700g) fresh or frozen peas
2 rashers of streaky bacon
1 small onion – finely chopped
2oz (50g) butter or vegetable fat spread
1 teaspoon sugar
pinch of grated nutmeg
salt & freshly ground pepper

1. Boil or steam peas for 3-5 minutes.

2. Fry bacon until crisp.

3. Melt butter or vegetable fat spread and sauté onion on low heat until transparent.

4. Toss peas, bacon and onion together and season to taste.

Turkey is delicious eaten with plain brussels sprouts & roast potatoes. Do not forget to buy cranberry sauce!

Christmas pudding

ingredients
preparation

6oz (175g) plain flour
2 teaspoons ground mixed spice
1 teaspoon ground cinnamon
half a teaspoon grated nutmeg
6oz(175g) fresh white breadcrumbs
6oz (175g) butter
6oz (175g) soft brown sugar
12oz (350g) sultanas
8oz (250g) raisins
8oz (250g) currants
3oz (75g) chopped mixed peel
2 eggs – beaten
grated juice & rind or 1 orange
quarter of a pint (150ml) ale or whisky
3 tablespoons brandy

instructions

1. Sift flour and spices into a bowl. Mix butter
   and flour until mixture becomes like breadrumbs.
   Add soft white breadcrumbs and stir in sugar.
   Add other ingredients and stir.

2. Turn into a greased 2.5 pint (1 litre) pudding basin

3. Cover with pudding cloth or greaseproof paper
   and foil. Steam for 6 hours in covered pan.

4. Top up with boiling water as necessary.

5. Cool and store in cool dry place for 3-4 months.

6. To serve, steam the pudding or 2 hours. Warm 3
   tablespoons brandy and ignite. Pour flaming brand
   over pudding. Top with sprig of holly. Serve with
   brandy butter or cream.

*optional

To re-steam a Christmas pudding with brandy butter

1 Christmas pudding
3 tablespoons brandy
1 sprig fresh holly

(BRANDY BUTTER)
8oz (225g) caster sugar
4oz (100g) unsalted butter
2 tablespoons brandy

1. To re-steam a cooked Christmas pudding. Steam for 1-2 hours. Cover pudding with double sheet of greaseproof paper and a sheet of silver foil. Tie in place with string.

2. Place pudding basin in steamer set over a pan of boiling water, or stand pudding basin on inverted saucer in a saucepan. With either method boiling water should come half way up the side of the pudding basin throughout the steaming process.

3. Top up with fresh boiling water during steaming. To serve turn pudding out onto serving dish.

4. Put a sprig of fresh holly into the top of the pudding. Heat 3 tablespoons of brandy in a saucepan. Remove from heat and light with match. The brandy will flare up briefly. Pour flaming brandy over the pudding. Serve immediately.

5. (BRANDY BUTTER) Cream butter and sugar until light and fluffy. Add brandy and beat in well. Keeps in fridge for 2 weeks, or can be frozen.

Chocolate roulade

Ingredients
Preparation

5 eggs
6oz (175g) *plain block chocolate*
half a pint (275ml) double cream
6oz (175g) *caster sugar*
icing sugar
burnt almonds for decoration
vanilla essence
rum or brandy
1 baking tin – lined with baking parchment paper

Instructions

1. Preheat oven to 180°C or 350°F or gas mark 4.

2. Melt chocolate and 1 tablespoon water in saucepan

3. Separate the eggs. Beat yolks and caster sugar in
   bowl until thick. Use hand held whisk with bowl
   set over a pan of boiling water. Or use a hand held
   electric whisk.

4. Beat egg whites until stiff and standing in peaks.

5. Pour melted chocolate over egg yolks. Whisk again
   Fold egg whites into egg yolks.

6. Pour into prepared baking tin. Bake in a preheated
   oven for 15-20 minutes, or until firm to the touch
   Leave to cool.

7. Put a sheet of greaseproof paper on table. Dust with
   icing sugar. Lay roulade on greaseproof paper. Strip
   greaseproof paper off the bottom of the roulade.

8. Cover two thirds of the roulade with whipped cream
   Gently roll up like a swiss roll. If mixture falls out
   shape mould it together. Lift roulade onto serving
   dish. Dust with icing sugar.

*optional

Miscellaneous
Salads

Caesar salad
Serves two

4 *slices thick white bread – crusts removed*
2 *cos lettuce hearts*
2 *red apples*
1 *teaspoon lemon juice*
4oz (100g) *parmesan cheese*
butter or vegetable fat spread
olive oil

(DRESSING)
1 *egg yolk*
3 *tablespoons olive oil*
1 *tablespoon white wine vinegar*
1 *teaspoon lemon juice*
2-3 *tablespoons single cream*
1 *teaspoon Dijon mustard*
1 *clove garlic – peeled & pressed**
salt & freshly ground pepper

1. To make the croutons, cut the bread into 0.5 inch (1CM) cubes. Heat butter or vegetable fat spread and oil in frying pan. Fry cubes of bread, until golden brown on both sides. Drain on absorbent kitchen paper.

2. Wash lettuce leaves and shake off excess water.

3. Cut apples in quarters. Remove core and seeds and slice. Toss in lemon juice.

4. (DRESSING) Mix olive oil, white wine vinegar, egg yolk, cream, mustard, lemon juice, parmesan and garlic.* Whisk until blended and season to taste.

5. Pour dressing over salad.

   Serve with grated parmesan cheese.

*optional

Cold chicken salad
Serves two/four

1 small chicken
2 green peppers – cut in small pieces
6 sticks celery – cut in thin slices
1 × 4oz (100g) tin sweetcorn
4 kiwi fruit – peeled & sliced
quarter of a pint (150ml) mayonnaise
half a teaspoon paprika
half a tablespoon soy sauce
1 tablespoon balsamic vinegar
2 tablespoons fresh parsley – freshly chopped
salt & freshly ground pepper
a few chives to garnish

1. Cover chicken with water. Bring to the boil and simmer for 1 hour. Leave chicken to cool in stock.

2. Remove chicken from stock and strip off flesh. Cut chicken flesh into bite sized pieces.

3. Re-boil carcass and skin in stock for 1 hour, strain and use as fresh chicken stock.

4. Mix chicken, vegetables, kiwi, paprika, soy sauce and balsamic vinegar and stir well. Mix in mayonnaise and parsley and season to taste.

Serve on bed of salad leaves. Sprinkle with chives.

Fresh stock may be decanted into small containers and frozen.

Coleslaw with blue cheese dressing Serves two/four

8oz (225g) white cabbage
8oz (225g) red cabbage
4oz (100g) carrots
1 eating apple
2oz (50g) sultanas

(BLUE CHEESE DRESSING)
2 oz (50g) blue cheese
2 tablespoons mayonnaise
1 tablespoon lemon juice
5oz (150g) plain yoghurt
salt & freshly ground pepper

1. Put cabbage, carrots and apple through slicing bla
   of food processor. Shred very fine.

2. Mix cheese, mayonnaise, yoghurt and lemon juice.
   Beat until smooth. Season to taste.

3. Add sultanas. Pour dressing over shredded vegetab
   Chill until ready to serve.

*optional

Green salad
Serves two/four

2 small gem lettuce hearts
sprigs of baby frisee
sprigs of lamb's lettuce
sprigs of watercress
fresh coriander, tarragon & flat-leaf parsley

(FRENCH DRESSING OR VINAIGRETTE)
olive oil
white wine vinegar
2 tablespoons of Dijon mustard
1 tablespoon sugar
half a teaspoon lemon juice
salt & freshly ground pepper
1 clean jam jar

1. Wash the lettuce under cold running water.

2. Transfer greens to a colander. Drain and spin dry.

3. Wrap greens and herbs in clean tea towel.
   Chill until ready to use.

4. (FRENCH DRESSING OR VINAIGRETTE) Put 2
   tablespoons Dijon mustard, 1 tablespoon sugar,
   half a teaspoon of lemon juice, salt and freshly
   ground pepper into a jam jar. Then fill jam jar with
   two thirds olive oil and one third white wine vinegar.
   Replace lid and shake well.

5. Place the greens in a serving bowl. Add a little
   dressing, toss through and serve.

   Keep French dressing in the fridge.

Parsnip & fennel salad
Serves two/four

redients
reparation

4 small parsnips
1 fennel bulb
2 tablespoons of fresh parsley
2 tablespoons vinaigrette dressing

ructions

1. Peel parsnips and cut into quarters.

2. Boil for 4 minutes until tender.

3. Cut fennel into rounds. Strip leaves off stalk. Put leaves in cup and cut with kitchen scissors. Chop parsley.

4. Combine parsnips and fennel. Pour vinaigrette dressing over vegetables and sprinkle with chopped parsley.

    See previous page (115) for vinaigrette dressing.

Prawn & cucumber salad Serves two

8oz (225g) peeled prawns
1 cucumber – thinly sliced
1 tablespoon salt
1 tablespoon sugar
3 tablespoons white wine vinegar
1oz (25g) sugar
2 teaspoon fresh or dried dill
2 tablespoons chopped fresh chives
quarter of a pint (150ml) carton sour cream
salt & freshly ground pepper

1. Peel and slice cucumber. Put in bowl with 1 tablespoon salt and 1 tablespoon sugar. Leave for 30 minutes.

2. Put vinegar, water and sugar in small saucepan and heat until sugar dissolves. Boil for 1 minute then remove from heat. Cool.

3. Put cucumber in colander to drain off liquid. Rinse under cold running water. Pat dry with absorbent kitchen paper.

4. Mix cucumber, prawns, dill and cold vinegar mixture. Cover and chill for 30 minutes.

5. Mix chives, dill and sour cream and season to taste.

6. Serve chilled salad with sour cream sauce, sprinkled with chopped chives.

Tomato salad
Serves two

1 lb (450g) tomatoes
2 tablespoons of fresh chopped parsley
juice of 2 lemons
3 tablespoons olive oil
1 tablespoon brown sugar
salt & freshly ground pepper
1 clove garlic*

1. Slice tomatoes.

2. Chop parsley and sprinkle over tomatoes.

3. Add lemon juice, olive oil, crushed garlic*
   and sugar and season to taste.

*optional

Miscellaneous Sauces

Bread sauce

ingredients
preparation

1 *onion*
1 *pint (575ml) milk*
4oz (100g) fresh breadcrumbs
1oz (25g) butter or vegetable fat spread
3 cloves
half a teaspoon nutmeg
salt & freshly ground pepper

instructions

1. Put onion and spices in milk and bring to boil.
   Leave to infuse for 30 minutes.

2. Strain milk into pan. Add breadcrumbs.
   Season to taste.

3. Gently reheat for 20 minutes until sauce thickens.

   Serve with roast chicken or turkey.

Cheese sauce

1.5oz (45g) butter
1.5oz (45g) plain flour
three quarters of a pint (425ml) milk
4oz (100g) cheddar cheese
2 teaspoons Dijon mustard
quarter of a teaspoon nutmeg

1. Melt butter or vegetable fat spread.

2. Add flour and blend in milk. Stir until smooth.

3. Add the cheese. Season to taste. Add Dijon mustard and nutmeg. Cool.

Hollandaise sauce

redients
reparation

2 *teaspoons lemon juice*
2 *teaspoons white wine vinegar*
2 *egg yolks*
4oz (100g) *unsalted butter*
salt & freshly ground pepper

structions

1. Put lemon juice and vinegar into a bowl and add e
   yolks. Place bowl over a saucepan of simmering wa
   and whisk until light and frothy.

2. Dice butter and add in small amounts, whisking a
   the butter is absorbed by the egg yolks. The mixtu
   will begin to thicken. Keep whisking all the time.

3. Season to taste and keep warm.

*optional

Mayonnaise

1-2 egg yolks
quarter to half a pint (150-275ml) olive oil
1-2 tablespoons of white wine vinegar
salt & freshly ground pepper
1-2 tablespoons of Dijon mustard
hand-held beater or electric beater

1. Separate egg yolks from whites. Put egg yolks in clean bowl and begin to whisk.

2. Add olive oil in a steady trickle until the mayonnaise starts to thicken. Whisk constantly and as mayonnaise thickens increase the flow of olive oil.

3. Season to taste and add Dijon mustard.

4. Add enough white wine vinegar to thin the mayonnaise.

5. If mayonnaise curdles, start again with a fresh egg yolk. Put fresh egg yolk in clean bowl and add curdled mixture in a gentle trickle. Whisk vigorously until mayonnaise thickens. It is not possible to rescue curdled mayonnaise once vinegar has been added.

This requires patience!

White sauce or Velouté sauce

*redients
reparation

2oz (50g) *butter or vegetable fat spread*
2oz (50g) *flour*
half to 1 pint (275-575ml) milk
half to 1 pint (275-575ml) stock
salt & freshly ground pepper

ructions

1. Melt butter or vegetable fat spread in saucepan over a low heat. Add flour. Use a wire whisk to st flour into the fat. Do not burn butter or vegetabl fat spread.

2. Remove from heat. Blend in milk, stirring until sauce thickens and is smooth.

3. Return to the heat. Sauce should coat the back of a wooden spoon. Season to taste.

   This is the foundation sauce. Add any flavouring to this base. Milk is used to make a WHITE SAUCE *and stock is used for a* VELOUTÉ SAUCE *base.*

Miscellaneous Soups

Borsch soup
Serves two/four

1 packet of beetroot (buy vacuum packed 4 to a packet)
quarter of a pint (150ml) carton of sour cream
1 pint (575ml) chicken stock (use vegetable stock
cube for vegetarians)
squeeze of lemon juice
chopped parsley to decorate
salt & freshly ground pepper

1. Liquidize three of the beetroots and add the stock.
   Season to taste and add lemon juice.

2. Grate the remaining beetroot and add to puréed
   beetroot. Simmer, but do not boil.

3. Decorate with chopped parsley and a swirl of
   sour cream.

Carrot soup
Serves two/four

1 lb (450g) carrots – peeled & chopped
1 onion – chopped
1 oz (25g) butter or vegetable fat spread
half to 1 pint (275-575ml) stock (use vegetable stock cube)
half a teaspoon grated nutmeg
1 tablespoon chopped chives
quarter of a pint (150ml) single cream
1 garlic clove*
salt & freshly ground pepper

1. Melt butter or vegetable fat spread and sauté onion until transparent.

2. Add carrots and garlic. Simmer 4 minutes.

3. Add stock and bring to the boil. Lower heat and simmer for 5-7 minutes. Season to taste.

4. Cool and pass through a mouli legume or purée in a food processor.

5. Stir in herbs and cream. Decorate with chopped chives and sour cream.

Cream of lemon chicken soup Serves two/four

2oz (50g) butter or vegetable fat spread
6 spring onions – sliced
4oz (100g) chicken breast – cut in tiny pieces
2 teaspoons tarragon
2 teaspoons lemon grass
1 oz (25g) plain flour
1 pint (575ml) vegetable or chicken stock (use stock cube
grated rind & juice of 1 lemon
2 teaspoons soy sauce
quarter of a pint (150ml) single cream
salt & freshly ground pepper

1. Melt butter or vegetable fat spread and sauté onion in covered saucepan for 5 minutes.

2. Add chicken pieces, tarragon and lemon grass. Cook on low heat for 5 minutes.

3. Stir in flour. Blend in stock, lemon rind, lemon juice and soy sauce. Cover and simmer until chicken is tender – about 5 minutes. Season to taste and leave to cool.

4. Stir in cream when soup is cold and reheat without boiling.

*optional

Potato & mushroom soup Serves two/four

1oz (25g) butter or vegetable fat spread
1 onion – chopped
1 clove of garlic – squeezed*
3 potatoes – peeled & diced
1lb (450g) mushrooms – sliced
1 pint (575ml) chicken stock (use vegetable stock
cube for vegetarians)
half a teaspoon dried herbs
quarter of a pint (150ml) single cream
3 tablespoons sherry*
half a teaspoon grated nutmeg
salt & freshly ground pepper

1. Melt butter or vegetable fat spread in large saucepan and sauté onion. Add potatoes and garlic.* Cook on a low heat for 5 minutes.

2. Add mushrooms and cook for 4 minutes. Add stock and herbs and season to taste. Bring to boil and simmer for 5-10 minutes.

3. Pass soup through sieve or liquidize in a food processor.

4. Return to pan and add cream, sherry, nutmeg, salt and pepper.

5. Reheat without boiling.

Try using sweet potatoes & a selection of mushrooms, either chestnut, portobello, shitake, field, button, or dried wild mushrooms.

Tomato & orange soup with croutons
Serves two/four

2oz (50g) *butter or vegetable fat spread*
1 *onion – peeled & sliced*
2lb (1kg) *tomatoes*
1 *stick of celery*
1 *clove of garlic**
1 *bay leaf*
juice & rind of 2 oranges
1-2 *teaspoons of sugar*
chopped parsley to garnish
2 *slices of bread*
salt & freshly ground pepper

1. Melt butter or vegetable fat spread in saucepan and sauté onion until transparent. Add tomatoes, celery garlic and bay leaf. Simmer for 10-15 minutes.

2. Purée soup in a food processor or pass through a sieve or mouli legume. Add orange juice, grated orange rind and sugar. Season to taste. Reheat, but do not boil once orange juice has been added.

3. (CROUTONS) Cut bread into 0.5 inch (1CM) cubes. Heat butter or vegetable fat spread in a frying pan Fry cubes of bread until golden brown on both sid Drain on absorbent kitchen paper.

   Serve with chopped parsley and croutons.

Vichyssoise soup
Serves two/four

2oz (50g) butter or vegetable fat spread
1lb (450g) leeks – washed & sliced
8oz (225g) potatoes – peeled & sliced
1 pint (575ml) stock (use vegetable stock cube)
half a pint (275ml) milk (or low fat)
quarter of a pint (150ml) cream
1 tablespoon chopped chives
salt & freshly ground pepper

1. Melt butter or vegetable fat spread and sauté leeks and potatoes on low heat for 7 minutes.

2. Add stock and bring to the boil. Simmer for 10 minutes.

3. Cool and pass through a sieve or food processor. Stir in milk and cream. Season to taste.

4. Chill and sprinkle with chopped chives.

   This soup is traditionally served cold, but is good served hot! Do not boil if cream has been added.

Winter soup
Serves four

half a turnip
half a swede
2 parsnips
4 carrots
2 potatoes
1 leek
1 onion
1 × 14oz (400g) tin of chopped tomatoes
2 pints (1 litre) of chicken stock (use vegetable stock
cube for vegetarians)
chopped fresh parsley
1 teaspoon worcester sauce
2oz (50g) pearl barley
salt & freshly ground pepper

1. Peel all vegetables into thin matchstick strips using the slicing blade of a food processor.

2. If using pearl barley soak and prepare. Follow instructions on packet.

3. Put shredded vegetables into saucepan. Cover with stock. Add tin of tomatoes and bring to the boil. Lower heat and simmer 5-10 minutes.

4. Season to taste. Add worcester sauce.

5. If using pearl barley add to vegetables. Top up with more stock if necessary.

6. Sprinkle with freshly chopped parsley.

   This nutritious soup can be made with any root vegetab
   The amount of stock used is up to the individual prefere

Miscellaneous
Store cupboard

Biscuits
(*plain & sweet*)
Breadcrumbs
Butter
Cereals
Cheese
Chocolate
(*plain*)
Cloves & dried herbs
(*chives, cloves, coriander,
cumin, cinnamon, garlic,
mixed herbs, nutmeg,
oregano, tarragon, curry
powder, & parsley*)
Coffee
Cornflour
Curry powder
Custard powder
Dried fruit
(*apricots, currants, dates,
figs, prunes, raisins &
sultanas*)
Dried pearl barley
Dried lentils
Dried split peas
Flour
(*plain & self-raising*)
Fruit
(*tins of fruit salad, peaches,
& pears*)
Fruit juice
Garlic
Jam
Jellies
(*packets*)
Lemon juice
Lasagne
Macaroni & spaghetti
Margarine
Marmalade

Mustards
(*English, Dijon & dried
mustard powder*)
Olive oil
Parmesan cheese
Pepper
(*freshly ground*)
Salt
(*normal & 'lo salt' reduced
sodium salt alternative*)
Sunflower oil
Rice
(*easy-cook & risotto*)
Salad cream
Soy sauce
Soups
(*tins of chicken, consommé,
mushroom, & tomato etc*)
Stock cubes
(*beef, chicken, & vegetable*)
Sugar
(*brown, caster, icing & white
sugar*)
Tea
Tomato ketchup
Vanilla essence
Vegetable fat spread
Tinned spinach
Tinned sweet-corn
Tinned tomatoes
Vinegar
(*balsamic, red & white wine*)
Worcester sauce

Miscellaneous Kitchen utensils

Apron
Baking parchment
Blender
Chopping board
Cake tin
Can opener
Carving knife
Cast-iron griddle pan
Clingfilm
Colander
Food processor
Frying pan
Grater
Greaseproof paper
Hand held electric mixer
Kettle
Kitchen paper
Kitchen scissors
Kitchen timer
Lemon squeezer
Large sieve
Liquidizer
Measuring jug
Metal skewer
Mouli-legumes
(*sieve with handle to purée vegetables*)
Omelette pan
Pastry brush
Pepper mill
Perforated metal spoon
Potato peeler
Pudding basins
(*small, medium & large*)
Rind zester
Roasting tins
Rolling pin

Saucepans
(*with lids*)
Scales
Sharp knives
(*of varying sizes*)
Silver foil
Sieve
Spatula
Vegetable masher
Whisk
(*manual & electric*)
Wok
Wooden cocktail sticks
Wooden spoons

Index

(v) denotes vegetarian

(v) denotes vegetarian

(v) denotes vegetarian

(v) denotes vegetarian

(v) denotes vegetarian

(v) denotes vegetarian